# AQA  Religious Studies A

## St Luke's Gospel

GCSE

**Francis Loftus**

Series editor

**Cynthia Bartlett**

Nelson Thornes

Published in 2009 by:
Nelson Thornes Ltd
Delta Place
27 Bath Road
CHELTENHAM
GL53 7TH
United Kingdom

09  10  11  12  13 / 10  9  8  7  6  5  4  3  2  1

A catalogue record for this book is available from the British Library

ISBN 978 1 4085 0459 8

Cover photograph: Rex Features

Illustrations by Paul McCaffrey (c/o Sylvie Poggio Artists Agency) and David Russell

Page make-up by Pantek Arts Ltd, Maidstone

Printed and bound in Spain by GraphyCems

## Acknowledgements

The author and publisher are grateful to the following for permissions to reproduce photographs and other copyright material:

**Text acknowledgements**

Scripture quotations taken from the Holy Bible, New International Version. Copyright © 1978, 1984 by International Bible Society. Used by permission of Hodder & Stoughton, a division of Hodder Headline Ltd. All rights reserved. 'NIV' is a registered trademark of International Bible Society. UK trademark number 1448790. Romerotrust.org.uk; motherteresa.org.

**Photo acknowledgements**

**Alamy:** 1.2A; 1.4A; 1.5A; 1.9A; 1.11A; 1.12B; 2.1B; 2.2A; 2.3A; 2.4A; 2.5A; 2.6A; 2.8A ; 2.9; 3.2B; 3.8B; 3.9B; 3.10B; 4.2B; 4.3A; 4.4A; 4.5A; 4.9A; 4.11A; 4.11B; 5.1A; 5.3B; 5.4A; 5.4B; 5.5B; 5.5A; 5.6A; 5.6B; 5.7A; 6.2A; 6.3A; 6.3B; 6.9A; 6.10A. **Art Archive:** 2.3B; 2.4A; 2.10A; 4.6A. **Art Directors:** 1.10A; 2.1A. **Bridgeman:** 1.4B. **Corbis:** 1.8; 1.11; 2.2; 3.1; 3.8; 6.5; 6.7. **Fotolia:** 1.6A; 2.3B; 3.3C; 3.4B; 3.7B. **Getty:** 1.12A. **iStockphoto:** 1.8B; 1.10A; 3.3B; 3.4A; 3.6A; 4.1A; 4.2A; 4.7A; 4.7B; 4.8A; 4.10B; 6.1A; 6.4A; 6.6A; 6.6B; 6.6C; 6.7B; 6.10A. **Rex Features:** 3.2A. **The Salvation Army:** 6.4B. **The Sylvia Wright Trust:** 1.12D. Special appreciation is offered to Elisabeth Savery and Frances Topp for photograph research.

Every effort has been made to contact the copyright holders and we apologise if any have been overlooked. Should copyright have been unwittingly infringed in this book, the owners should contact the publishers, who will make corrections at reprint.

# Contents

Nelson Thornes has worked in partnership with AQA to make sure that this book offers you the best possible support for your GCSE course. All the content has been approved by the senior examining team at AQA, so you can be sure that it gives you just what you need when you are preparing for your exams.

## ◾ How to use this book

This book covers everything you need for your course.

### Learning Objectives

At the beginning of each section or topic you'll find a list of Learning Objectives based on the requirements of the specification, so you can make sure you are covering everything you need to know for the exam.

| Objectives |
|---|
| Objectives |
| Objectives |
| Objectives |
| First objective. |
| Second objective. |

### AQA Examiner's Tips

Don't forget to look at the AQA Examiner's Tips throughout the book to help you with your study and prepare for your exam.

> **AQA Examiner's tip**
>
> Don't forget to look at the AQA Examiner's Tips throughout the book to help you with your study and prepare for your exam.

### AQA Examination-style Questions

These offer opportunities to practise doing questions in the style that you can expect in your exam so that you can be fully prepared on the day.

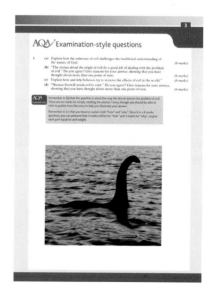

AQA examination questions are reproduced by permission of the Assessment and Qualifications Alliance.

# AQA GCSE St Luke's Gospel

This book is written specifically for GCSE students following the AQA Religious Studies Specification A, *Unit 6: St Luke's Gospel*. It covers Luke's account of Jesus' life and teaching in first century CE, the background to his ministry, and the significance of Jesus for Christians as seen by Luke. Only material in Luke's Gospel will be examined.

It is important that you learn the set Bible passages. These are included in the text. You must also understand all Key Terms: look for the Key Term boxes or use the Glossary to locate the explanations. The Link boxes will help you to cross refer from spread to spread to find to additional material that will add to your understanding of the topics.

## ■ Topics in this unit

In the examination you will be asked to answer five questions out of six that are based on the following topics:

### Background to Luke's Gospel

This topic examines what led to Luke writing his gospel, the nature and purpose of Luke's Gospel, and its meaning and importance for Christians in the 1st century and the 21st century.

### Salvation

This topic examines salvation as the central theme of Jesus' teaching. You will study the stories surrounding the birth of Jesus and the significance of this event for Christians.

### The authority of Jesus

This topic examines how Jesus gained power from the Holy Spirit, which enabled him to perform miracles. You will study how the titles used of Jesus show him to be the Messiah.

### The suffering, death and resurrection of Jesus

This topic covers the arrest and trials of Jesus, his crucifixion and resurrection, and how his appearances after the resurrection support his Messianic claim.

### Universalism

This topic considers the way Jesus cared for those on the fringes of Jewish society, including gentiles, sinners and women. You will study his teaching that God's love is for all people.

### Discipleship

This topic looks at stories and teachings about the Twelve, and parables about discipleship. It also looks at prayer in the Christian life and the demands of discipleship today.

## ■ Assessment guidance

Each chapter has an assessment guidance section to allow you to test your knowledge and understanding. There are short-answer questions worth from one to three marks, and longer questions worth up to six marks that test your ability to retell texts. There are also questions that test your ability to give your opinion or argue differing viewpoints, and these carry either three or six marks. To help you understand what examiners are looking for, there are also sample answers for you to mark. The mark schemes below will help you.

*Examination questions will test two assessment objectives:*

| AO1 | Describe, explain and analyse, using knowledge and understanding. | 50% |
|---|---|---|
| AO2 | Use evidence and reasoned argument to express and evaluate personal responses, informed insights, and differing viewpoints. | 50% |

The examiner will also take into account the quality of your written communication – how clearly you express yourself and how well you communicate your meaning. The grid below also gives you some guidance on the sort of quality examiners expect to see at different levels.

## Levels of response mark scheme for six-mark evaluation questions

| Levels | Criteria for AO1 | Criteria for AO2 | Quality of written communication | Marks |
|---|---|---|---|---|
| 0 | Nothing relevant or worthy of credit | An unsupported opinion or no relevant evaluation | The candidate's presentation, spelling, punctuation and grammar seriously obstruct understanding | 0 marks |
| Level 1 | Something relevant or worthy of credit | An opinion supported by simple reason | The candidate presents some relevant information in a simple form. The text produced is usually legible. Spelling, punctuation and grammar allow meaning to be derived, although errors are sometimes obstructive | 1 mark |
| Level 2 | Elementary knowledge and understanding, e.g. two simple points | An opinion supported by one developed reason or two simple reasons | | 2 marks |
| Level 3 | Sound knowledge and understanding | An opinion supported by one well developed reason or several simple reasons. N.B. Candidates who make no religious comment should not achieve more than Level 3 | The candidate presents relevant information in a way which assists with the communication of meaning. The text produced is legible. Spelling, punctuation and grammar are sufficiently accurate not to obscure meaning | 3 marks |
| Level 4 | A clear knowledge and understanding with some development | An opinion supported by two developed reasons with reference to religion | | 4 marks |
| Level 5 | A detailed answer with some analysis, as appropriate | Evidence of reasoned consideration of two different points of view, showing informed insights and knowledge and understanding of religion | The candidate presents relevant information coherently, employing structure and style to render meaning clear. The text produced is legible. Spelling, punctuation and grammar are sufficiently accurate to render meaning clear | 5 marks |
| Level 6 | A full and coherent answer showing good analysis, as appropriate | A well-argued response, with evidence of reasoned consideration of two different points of view showing informed insights and ability to apply knowledge and understanding of religion effectively | | 6 marks |

**Note:** In evaluation (AO2) answers to questions worth only 3 marks, the first three levels apply. Questions which are marked out of 3 marks do not ask for two views, but reasons for your own opinion.

Successful study of this unit will result in a Short Course GCSE award. Study of one further unit will provide a Full Course GCSE award. Other units in Specification A which may be taken to achieve a Full Course GCSE award are:

- Unit 1  Christianity
- Unit 2  Christianity: Ethics
- Unit 3  Roman Catholicism
- Unit 4  Roman Catholicism: Ethics
- Unit 7  Philosophy of Religion
- Unit 8  Islam
- Unit 9  Islam: Ethics
- Unit 10  Judaism
- Unit 11  Judaism: Ethics
- Unit 12  Buddhism
- Unit 13  Hinduism
- Unit 14  Sikhism

N.B. Units 5 and 6 are a prohibited combination, so for a Full Course qualification you may not study both St Mark's Gospel (Unit 5) and St Luke's Gospel (Unit 6).

# 1 Background to St Luke's Gospel

## 1.1 What is a gospel?

### Gospel truth

'But it's gospel, sir!' The pupil who wants the teacher to believe that what she is telling him is true and should not be doubted says this, but does she really know what she is saying? The word 'gospel' has acquired this sense over the centuries, but it actually has a meaning of its own.

'Gospel' literally means 'good news'. It is a word used by the Christian Church to refer to the teachings of Jesus and the apostles. There are four gospels in the New Testament: Matthew, Mark, Luke and John. These gospels were included in the New Testament because they were judged to be good accounts of the life and teaching of Jesus.

### The New Testament gospels

The gospels in the New Testament are a distinctive kind of writing. They contain stories about the life and teachings of Jesus, told by people with faith in him. The gospels were written with a particular group of Christians in mind, not only to give them an idea of the preaching and activities of Jesus but also to support their faith.

### The oral tradition

Almost from the beginning, Christians were persecuted for claiming that Jesus was the Messiah and had risen from the dead. First they were persecuted by the Jews, but soon the Romans, who were generally tolerant of different cults and religions, became involved too. The gospel stories, particularly the resurrection story, were circulated to give the early believers hope.

The stories were passed round orally among groups of Christians in Jerusalem and the near east. They would have included Jesus' teachings and the accounts of his miracles. Most important, though, were the stories of his last week on earth and his arrest, trial, crucifixion and resurrection. That Jesus died and rose from the dead was the essence of the gospel, and was the good news that the persecuted early Christians wanted to share.

Eyewitnesses to Jesus' life and work would have been important in the oral tradition because they could explain to others what they had seen and experienced firsthand.

**Objectives**

Understand the nature of the New Testament.

Know and understand the meaning of the term 'gospel'.

Understand the nature of Luke's Gospel and its place in the New Testament.

**Key terms**

Gospel: literally 'good news'; there are four gospels telling of the life and work of Jesus.

AQA **Examiner's tip**

Learn the meaning of the word 'gospel'.

## The gospel texts

Gradually, eyewitnesses began to die out. There was a need to write down the stories or they might be lost forever.

The gospels were written some time after Jesus died (some believe around 33 CE). Mark is regarded as the first gospel, written around 64 to 70 CE; Luke follows between 70 and 90 CE; then Matthew in 85 to 110 CE and John in 90 to 120 CE.

**A**   *The main places in Israel referred to by Luke. Jesus was born in Bethlehem; he was taken to Jerusalem as a child and then brought up in Galilee. His ministry began there. Israel at the time was part of the Roman Empire*

**Discussion activity**

1   Discuss in a group whether something written 30 to 90 years after the events it describes can be historically accurate.

a   What could have happened to the stories as they were told and retold?

b   Some people have suggested that the stories could have become exaggerated. Why would the early Christians exaggerate?

c   If some of the stories in the gospels became exaggerated, does this make them less valuable to the believers?

d   Discuss with your teacher why there are differences between the gospels.

**Research activity**

There are many other 'gospels'. Find out the names of some of them and, if possible, have a look at the texts to see how different they are.

**Summary**

You should now understand what a gospel is and know about the variety of sources Luke used.

## The synoptic gospels

The Gospel of Luke is one of the synoptic gospels. The synoptic gospels – Matthew, Mark and Luke – are very similar, but not the same. Each gospel has its own characteristics. For example, Mark seems to be very 'breathless' and urgent. In Matthew, there is a great emphasis on Jesus' teachings and miracles and the title Son of David, and the gospel is arranged like parts of the Old Testament. Luke is much more interested in history and trying to understand theology and tries to explain what the early Christians can learn about God from the life of Jesus.

## The writing of Luke's Gospel

The Gospel of Luke is the first of two books in the New Testament written by the same author. The other is the Acts of the Apostles, which continues the story, beginning with Jesus' ascension to heaven.

The writer of the Gospel of Luke had several sources for his knowledge, including the recollections of eyewitnesses, such as the disciples and the women who were with Jesus during his life. There were probably also written versions of some of their stories that were passed around the early church.

### Sources

A **source** is a document or tradition from which an author gets information. The importance of any historical document depends on the reliability of its sources. The closer a source is to an event, the more likely it is to be accurate and reliable. However, it is important to take into account whether a source could be biased in any way or might be seeking to put across a particular viewpoint.

Usually three sources are identified for the written version of Luke's Gospel:

- Mark's Gospel
- Q (Quelle)
- L (material found only in Luke's Gospel).

### Mark's Gospel

Almost all of Mark's Gospel is in Luke. Mark's Gospel is thought to have been written first, although Luke is likely to have seen it and copied from it. Scholars believe that Luke used Mark rather than the other way around because Luke extends the information given in Mark. Mark's Gospel gave Luke access to the memories of Peter, one of Mark's main sources.

### Q

Q stands for *Quelle*, the German word for 'source'. A theory that some of the things Jesus said were written down and circulated in the early church was developed to explain the similarities in the synoptic gospels, particularly those between Matthew and Luke when they have material that is not in Mark. This written source is known as Q. Scholars disagree on the precise content of Q, but the bulk of it is thought to comprise sayings of Jesus and some of his parables.

## L

Many passages in Luke do not appear in any other gospel and are thought to come from his own sources. More than a third of the gospel is L material.

L has some of the most important passages of the gospel:

- The Call of the Disciples (5:1–11)
- The Sinful Woman (7:36–50)
- Martha and Mary (10:38–42)
- The Widow of Nain (7:11–17)
- The Parable of the Good Samaritan (10:25–37)
- The Parable of the Persistent Neighbour (11:5–8)
- The Parable of the Lost Son (Forgiving Father) (15:1–2,11–32)
- The Parable of the Rich Man and Lazarus (16:19–31)
- The Parable of the Pharisee and the Tax Collector (18:9–14).

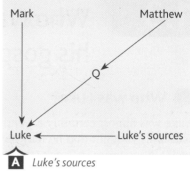

**A** *Luke's sources*

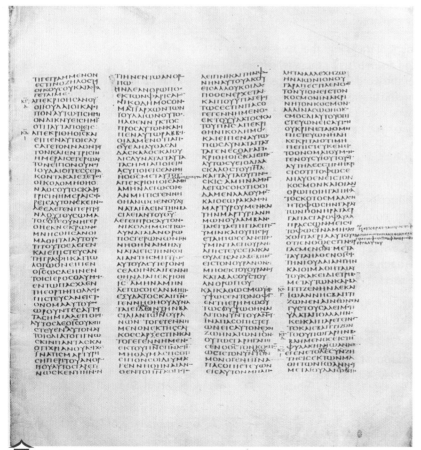

**B** *The Codex Sinaiticus, a 4th-century CE bible text written in Greek*

**Summary**

You should now understand what a source is, and know about the variety of sources that Luke used.

# Who was Luke and why did he write his gospel?

## Who was Luke?

Luke was almost certainly a Gentile (non-Jewish) Christian, and it is usually thought that he may have been Greek. Luke was clearly well able to write in Greek (the Greek he uses in the gospel is more advanced than that used by Mark or Matthew).

The earliest tradition, from the end of the 2nd century CE, says that Luke was a physician who spent time with Paul on his missionary journeys. In the New Testament Luke is referred to as the 'beloved physician' (Colossians 4:14), and is described as a 'fellow worker' of Paul (Philemon 24) who was 'with Paul' while he was awaiting trial (2 Timothy 4:11).

Later traditions suggest that Luke was a painter, and that he died at the age of 84, unmarried and without children.

## Why did Luke write his Gospel?

### Beliefs and teachings

Many have undertaken to draw up an account of the things that have been fulfilled among us, just as they were handed down to us by those who from the first were eyewitnesses and servants of the word. Therefore, since I myself have carefully investigated everything from the beginning, it seemed good also to me to write an orderly account for you most excellent Theophilus, so that you may know the certainty of the things you have been taught.

*Luke* 1:1–4

The Gospel of Luke was dedicated to the mysterious Theophilus. The name means 'lover of God'. In the introduction to the Gospel (Luke 1:1–4) the author states that he wants to 'compile an account of the things by those who were eyewitnesses and servants of the word'. He is anxious to stress that Theophilus knows what happened because of the evidence of eyewitnesses, and this approach has made most scholars believe that Luke, the author, was a historian.

When the Gospel first started circulating, it may have been anonymous. Gradually it was ascribed to Luke and this has remained the Church's teaching.

Luke's Gospel was meant to be shared amongst Christians and non-Christians across the Roman Empire to make Christianity attractive.

### Salvation history

The Jews believed that God intervened in history to save them from time to time – **salvation history**. For Luke there was no doubt that salvation has come through the work of Jesus. Because Luke believed that God had a plan for everyone, and not just the Jews, there is an emphasis in his gospel on women, Gentiles, the poor and children, and on other outsiders and those who are oppressed.

### Objectives

Develop knowledge of the authorship of Luke's Gospel.

Identify the main reasons why the Gospel was written.

### Key terms

**Salvation history**: the story of Jesus is presented from the perspective of faith in him as sent by God to save humanity.

### Discussion activity

Discuss whether knowing who wrote the Gospel is important.

**A** *Palestine is the time of Jesus*

## links

There is a more detailed discussion on the opening of Luke's Gospel on page 24.

## The second coming of Jesus (The Parousia)

The early Christians believed that Jesus would return to judge the world. They expected it to be soon after his resurrection and ascension to heaven. This expected second coming was also known as the Parousia.

However, by the end of the 1st century it was clear to them that this second coming was not going to happen quickly. It was therefore important to get Jesus' message written down before the eyewitnesses all died out.

## Prayer

Luke showed that prayer is essential to the Christian life. Jesus is often described as praying or as having prayed before making important decisions, and he taught his disciples to pray and encouraged them to do so. In the Garden of Gethsemane, just before his arrest, Jesus is described as praying with great intensity. Those who felt persecuted and oppressed will have been encouraged to pray in difficult times.

## The Holy Spirit

The Holy Spirit is the power behind the actions of Jesus and the disciples in Luke. Jesus is often described as having the Holy Spirit with him – for example, at his baptism and on his return to Galilee in Luke 3 and 4. The birth of John the Baptist is also linked to the Holy Spirit.

## Jesus the prophet

The Old Testament prophets were keen to spread the word of God, and taught people to follow the Law and the covenant. Luke is anxious to show that Jesus is a prophet like those in the Old Testament. Jesus spoke about the spirit of the Lord being upon him (Luke 4:18, quoting Isaiah), the sign of a prophet. Justice was a strong element in the teaching of the prophets, and this is reflected in Jesus' teaching, as is concern for the outcast. There is an almost exact parallel between Jesus' healing of the son of the widow of Nain and the healing of the widow of Zarephath by Elijah in the Old Testament, and in his work to help the oppressed Jews similar to prophets such as Amos.

**B** *Catacombs where Christians hid in Rome*

**Activities**

1. Why was it important for Luke to write what the eyewitnesses knew?
2. Why was it important that he wrote it when he did?
3. Explain the meaning of the name Theophilus.
4. How does praying help people when they feel they are in trouble?

**Research activity**

Look up the story of the healing of the widow of Zarephath by Elijah in I Kings 17:7–24 and compare it with the story of the widow of Nain in Luke 7:11–17.

**Summary**

You will now know some information about Luke, and understand Luke's reasons for writing the gospel and how the oppressed could draw strength from it.

# Jewish religious groups in the time of Jesus (1)

## Palestine in the time of Jesus

Jesus lived in Palestine at the beginning of the 1st century CE. There was a Roman Governor, and Roman troops were a regular sight in the land. King Herod the Great was a puppet ruler of the Romans. He had been put into power by them and they expected him to do their will.

Most scholars favour 4/5 BCE for the date of Jesus' birth and 33 CE for his death. He lived and worked mostly in the Galilee region but we are told in the gospel that he went to Samaria and ended his work in Jerusalem. Jesus was in many ways similar to other teachers living at this time. He travelled, he drew the crowds, he taught and he worked miracles.

Jesus came into contact with many different groups and often argued with them. This was not unusual – when people had new ideas or wanted action, they would speak in public and others would put forward conflicting points of view.

### Objectives

Know and understand about some of the religious groups in 1st-century Palestine.

Understand why Jesus came into conflict with these groups.

∞ links

For a definition of Hebrew, see page 140.

**A** Roman remains in 1st-century Palestine

## The Pharisees

The most powerful religious group at this time were the Pharisees. They were not priests and did not work in the Temple, but the people believed that the Pharisees were able to understand and interpret the Law (Torah).

Although they disliked the Romans, the Pharisees did not advocate the use of violence to overthrow them.

## The Law

The written part of the Law (Torah) consisted of the first five books of the Hebrew scriptures: Genesis, Exodus, Leviticus, Numbers and Deuteronomy. The oral part of the Law had been worked out over the centuries to try to show people how they should live, and was known as the halakhah. (This Hebrew word comes from the verb 'to walk' which gives the idea of 'walking in faith'.) There were 613 commandments in the Law but many more rules had been added since the Law was first written down. The Pharisees saw it as their role to interpret the Torah, to advise those who needed to understand the Law, to act as judges and to ensure that the Law was respected.

## Jesus and the Pharisees

Jesus frequently came into contact with the Pharisees. He would have joined in their debates and argued about the things they argued about. Indeed, Jesus' style in the Gospels is such that some Jewish scholars believe that he would have been regarded as a Pharisee in all but name.

Jesus' relationship with the Pharisees varied. They agreed, for example, on the belief that there was a life after death. They also agreed that there would be a judgement after death, with the righteous going to heaven and the wicked being punished. The Pharisees believed that the Kingdom of God would finally come – the messianic age.

At Jesus' baptism (Luke 3:21–22), a voice is described as coming from heaven saying, 'You are my beloved Son, with you I am well pleased.' For the Pharisees at that time, this would have been proof of Jesus' claims to be the Messiah.

**B**   *Jesus and the Pharisees*

### Activities

1   How did the Pharisees think they were helping people to live out the Law?

2   Read Luke 11:37–44 and make a list of the criticisms that Jesus made of the Pharisees.

3   Jesus called the Pharisees hypocrites. Look up the background to the word 'hypocrite'. What does it mean?

4   The Pharisees have the reputation of putting the Law before the needs of people. Are there any circumstances in which this is the right thing to do?

5   'Jesus would have been better keeping the Pharisees on his side.' What do you think? Give reasons for your answer.

### Summary

You will now have considered the role of the Pharisees and their beliefs and understood Jesus' relationship with them.

AQA   *Examiner's tip*

Remember that the Law included the written law and the customs that the Jews followed.

# 1.5 Jewish religious groups in the time of Jesus (2)

## The Sadducees

The Sadducees were largely upper class. They had very good links with the priestly families, but tended to be remote from ordinary people. They were not as influential as the Pharisees.

The Sadducees did not believe in the oral law and they argued with the Pharisees on a whole range of matters including divorce and ritual purity. They accepted only what was in the Pentateuch (the first five books of the Jewish Bible) as correct, and therefore did not believe in life after death. They argued with Jesus about this in Luke 20:27–49, where they asked him a question about whose wife a woman would be in heaven if she had married seven husbands.

## The Zealots

One of the groups that might have found Jesus very interesting were the Zealots. Indeed, Simon the Zealot is included in the list of disciples named in Luke 6:15. The Zealots would have heard Jesus teaching about justice and about the future Kingdom of God, and might have found this very attractive. They might have interpreted his teaching as challenging the rule of the Romans. They might also have been very impressed by Jesus' action in the Cleansing of the Temple (Luke 19:45–6).

The term 'Zealot' covers a wide range of small revolutionary groups in the area in the 1st century CE. They were committed to getting rid of the Romans in Palestine, by force if necessary. One Zealot group were the 'sicarii'. They carried a small knife (a 'sica'), which they would use to murder people in the crowd. If they were caught with this knife – whether they had used it or not – they could be put to death under Roman law.

One of the theories about why Judas Iscariot handed Jesus over to the authorities is that he, like the Zealot revolutionaries, thought that if Jesus were put face to face with the Romans he would start a war. (Some scholars believe that Judas may have been a member of the sicarii and suggest that the name 'Iscariot' could come from the same root.)

Such a war between the Zealots and the Romans did start in 66 CE, and the final stronghold of the Zealot forces was at Masada in the south of the country. There the revolutionaries chose to commit suicide rather than surrender to the Romans. This was not an uncommon thing for Jews to do when they believed their faith was being threatened.

### Objectives

Learn about important groups in Jesus' time in addition to the Pharisees.

 links

For a definition of Zealots, see the Glossary, page 141.

### Activity

1 Read the passage Luke 20:27–47:

a Do you think Jesus' answer to the Sadducees is a good one?

b What do you think it shows about beliefs in life after death?

c What could persecuted Christians gain from this incident?

### Discussion activity

1 Discuss with your teacher or in groups:

a The Roman law allowed for people to be put to death for the intention to murder, simply because they were carrying a knife. Is this a reasonable law? Give reasons for your opinion.

b The Jews were prepared to commit suicide rather than surrender. What does this show about their commitment and faith?

## The priests

The priests lived around Jerusalem and controlled the Temple. They ensured that sacrifices and festivals took place at the right time. The most senior priests had to work with the Romans and King Herod as the ruler of the Jews.

The priests were assisted by the Levites. Two of these are key characters in the Parable of the Good Samaritan.

In Luke, Jesus is not shown as having had much to do with the priests until he was on trial in the High Priest's house.

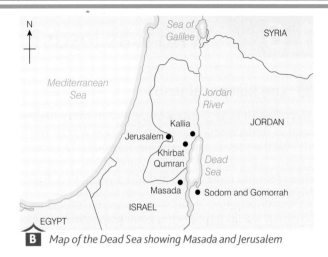

**B** *Map of the Dead Sea showing Masada and Jerusalem*

**A** *The stronghold at Masada*

## ∞links

For more on the Parable of the Good Samaritan see page 110.

For more on the Parable of the Good Samaritan see page 110.

### AQA Examiner's tip

You will not be asked to explain in detail about these groups in an examination, but you can refer to them when answering questions about conflict situations that Jesus faced.

### Discussion activity

2 In pairs, or a group, discuss how Jesus should have dealth with the Zealots as revolutionaries.

### Summary

You will now understand the different roles of three other groups that Jesus would have come into contact with: the Sadducees, the Zealots and the priests.

# 1.6 Who was Jesus?

## The historical Jesus

According to Luke, Jesus was the son of Mary and Joseph. He was born in Bethlehem, visited Jerusalem as a very young child and spent his childhood and early teens in Nazareth. His cousin was John the Baptist. Jesus appears to have done all the normal things that a boy of his age would have done, including going to Jerusalem at the age of twelve.

Nazareth would have been a good place for Jesus to grow up. It wasn't a very important city, but he would have had the chance to meet many foreigners and traders and this would have made him aware of different types of people. He was clearly traditionally educated in Hebrew because he was able to read and interpret the scrolls in the synagogue.

**Objectives**

Understand who Jesus was.

**Key terms**

**Saviour:** Christians believe that in his life and death, Jesus set people free from the power of evil and sin.

**A** *Bethlehem – Jesus' birthplace according to Luke*

## Matters of faith

The above is a very simple and straightforward way of explaining who Jesus was as far as the historical facts are concerned. However, as we are dealing with matters of faith as well as history, things are clearly not as simple as that.

If you read Luke chapters 1 and 2, you will see at once that there were a great number of unusual aspects surrounding Jesus' birth. They include the following:

- Elizabeth gave birth to John (the Baptist) after Zechariah had had a vision in the Temple.
- Gabriel, the messenger from God, came and told Mary that she was to give birth (the annunciation).

∞ **links**

For more on the annunciation and the birth stories, see Chapter 2.

- Mary was told by Gabriel that her son would be the 'Son of the Most High'.
- Joseph took Mary to Bethlehem, the expected birth place of the Messiah, where her baby was born.
- Angels told shepherds that a **Saviour** was born, and the shepherds visited Mary, Joseph and the baby in Bethlehem.

Some of these will be studied in more detail later in the book.

## ■ The life of Jesus

From the beginning, the readers of Luke are told that Jesus is the Son of God, yet it seems that his adult life was mostly that of a teacher. He began his ministry with the baptism of John and then spent some time (probably about three years) teaching, preaching, challenging those in authority and performing miracles.

He was to suffer for his beliefs. He was then arrested, tortured and crucified in Jerusalem. We are told by the gospel writer that on the Sunday morning the women found the tomb empty, and later Jesus is described as appearing to two disciples on the road to Emmaus.

So the life of Jesus is shown to be a mixture of the ordinary and the miraculous. He was a teacher and preacher, but there were occasions when he was involved in dramatic events and religious experiences – examples of this are the transfiguration and, most importantly, the resurrection.

**B**  *The traditional view of the birth of Jesus for many Christians*

∞ links

For more on the transfiguration, see Chapter 3. For more on the Resurrection, see Chapter 4.

AQA   *Examiner's tip*

Throughout your study of the Gospel of Luke, you need to be considering and remembering ways in which different people recognised Jesus as the Messiah.

**Extension activity**

Do some research on the evidence for the existence of Jesus, apart from what is in the New Testament.

**Research activity**

Find out what the Jewish historian Josephus wrote about who Jesus was.

**Discussion activity**

Discuss with your teacher what the phrase 'Son of God' might mean.

**Activities**

1. When Jesus was twelve he was taken to Jerusalem. Look up Luke 2:41–52. What does this event teach about who Jesus was? Imagine you were Mary or Joseph in this situation. What feelings would you have?

2. 'Jesus' relationship with God was the most important thing to him.' Do you agree? Give reasons for your answer.

3. How does Luke emphasise that Jesus was not just another Jewish teacher?

4. What would it mean to believers if they could not prove some of the information in the life of Jesus found in Luke?

**Summary**

You will now know who Jesus was and understand that Luke regarded Jesus as the Messiah, the Son of God.

# 1.7 The authority of Jesus

## Sources of Jesus' authority

Luke was keen to show that Jesus was the Son of God. The early Christians also claimed that this was true.

As the Son of God, Jesus would have greater **authority** than other teachers. There are a number of sources for this authority, including his fulfilment of the scriptures and his recognition by others with whom he came into contact.

### Fulfilment of the scriptures

After Jesus was baptised, he spent forty days in the wilderness. While he was there he was tempted by the Devil, who was trying to persuade him to take the easy route to success.

Jesus then returned to Nazareth. He had clearly been active in this area already because Luke 4:14–15 talks about a 'report concerning him' going around the countryside.

> " *He went to Nazareth, where he had been brought up, and on the Sabbath day he went into the synagogue, as was his custom. And he stood up to read. The scroll of the prophet Isaiah was handed to him. Unrolling it, he found the place where it is written:*
>
> *'The Spirit of the Lord is on me,*
> *because he has anointed me*
> *to preach good news to the poor.*
> *He has sent me to proclaim freedom for the prisoners*
> *and recovery of sight for the blind,*
> *to release the oppressed,*
> *to proclaim the year of the Lord's favour.'*
>
> *Then he rolled up the scroll, gave it back to the attendant and sat down. The eyes of everyone in the synagogue were fastened on him, and he began by saying to them, 'Today this scripture is fulfilled in your hearing.* "
>
> *Luke* 4:16–21

In this passage Jesus was in the synagogue reading and speaking about himself. He had experienced baptism and felt that he was called by God to preach the word of God.

Having recognised that the words he read from the prophet Isaiah applied to him, Jesus claimed that he fulfilled this prophecy about the Messiah. Isaiah had prophesied that the Messiah would come empowered by the spirit of God, and that people's lives would be transformed.

**Objectives**

Understand the basis of Jesus' authority.

See how others recognised Jesus' authority.

**Key terms**

**Authority**: power to give orders to others and expect obedience.

∞ links

For more on Jesus' temptations, see Chapter 3.

AQA **Examiner's tip**

In answering any question about Jesus' teaching or miracles, refer to his authority coming from God.

**A** *Jesus teaching in the synagogue*

**Activities**

1   On what did Jesus base his claim to authority?

2   Why was Jesus' authority rejected by those in the synagogue?

3   'Without his belief in God, Jesus would not have had the courage to act with the authority that he did.' Do you agree? Give reasons for your answer.

4   As you work through the Gospel of Luke, notice and make a list of all the occasions that Jesus' authority is recognised by others.

## Recognition by others

Jesus was recognised from the beginning as being special. In the birth stories the shepherds, Simeon and Anna, recognised him as one sent from God (Luke 2), who would bring salvation to Israel.

Later in the Gospel, at the baptism, there was the voice from heaven (Luke 3:22), saying: 'You are my Son, whom I love.' At the transfiguration (Luke 9:35) the voice is heard again and states: 'This is my Son, my Chosen; listen to him.' On these occasions the voice of God is shown as recognising Jesus' authority.

Sometimes in the Gospel it is other people who recognise Jesus. The Roman centurion, a Gentile, recognised that Jesus was able to cure his slave even without seeing him (Luke 7:7). Legion (or Mob) recognised Jesus as the 'Son of the Most High God' (Luke 8:28). The disciples recognised Jesus' authority when he calmed the storm (Luke 8:25), even though it led them to ask, 'Who is this?'

**Research activity**

Find out about the importance of a synagogue to a Jewish community, especially what was needed before one could be created.

**Summary**

You should now understand that Jesus' authority was based on scripture and recognised by others in the things that he said and did.

# The persecution of the Christians in the 1st century CE

## ▨ The Jews

Around 35 CE the early Christians were part of the Jewish faith and worshipped in the Temple and the synagogues. However, once the Christians decided to admit **Gentiles** the Jewish authorities turned against them and they were arrested. Many Christians then left Jerusalem and began to travel around the countries near Palestine.

During the Roman War in Palestine from 66 to 74 CE, the Christians would not fight on the side of the Jews. This led to a further split, and after the war the Jews banned Christians from the synagogues.

### The conversion of Paul

Saul, a Pharisee, was determined to root out the Christians and kill them. He was on his way to Damascus, in Syria, when he had a vision of Jesus and heard a voice asking why he was persecuting Jesus. He became blind as a result of this vision and was led to Damascus, where he met Ananias, a Christian. Ananias laid his hands on Saul and his sight returned. This was a sign that God had chosen Saul to spread the gospel. Following this incident, Saul became known as Paul and spent the rest of his life as a missionary sharing the news of Jesus and converting people.

## ▨ The Romans

As long as the Christians were worshipping with the Jews they were regarded as part of Judaism and tolerated by the Romans. However, they began to lose their protection as more and more Gentiles joined them. Jewish Christians had been exempted from Emperor Worship as Jews, but by 52 CE Christianity was no longer a distinctive Jewish group (a Roman historian writing at the end of the 1st century CE), and Suetonius reported that the Christians were expelled from Rome for creating disturbances.

### Persecution under Nero 64–68 CE

The Roman historian Tacitus wrote about how Nero tortured Christians after there was a rumour that they had started a fire in Rome. He describes some of the ways in which they died:

- They were covered in the skins of wild animals and torn to death by dogs.
- They were crucified.
- They were set on fire and used as torches in Nero's garden when it was dark.

Tacitus said that the public began to feel sorry for the Christians because they had done no wrong, but that Nero's cruelty needed satisfying. According to Christian tradition, both Peter and Paul died in this persecution.

## Persecution under Domitian 81–96 CE

The Roman Emperor Domitian is said to have persecuted Christians during his reign, but there is debate among historians about the extent of this persecution. According to one story, Domitian's cousin Flavius Clemens and his wife Domitilla were arrested because it was alleged that they had 'slipped into Jewish customs'. In other words, Domitilla had become a good Christian, and was no longer worshipping the many Roman gods. He was certainly regarded as a Christian martyr by the later church.

**A**   *The Colosseum in Rome where Christians were killed for their faith*

## The support of the gospel

The gospel, along with other books in the New Testament, could have given the early Christians hope in difficult times.

- Jesus demonstrated God's power by saving people from their illnesses. God would save those facing death and torture.
- There is the promise of resurrection for those who die for their faith.
- Pontius Pilate was shown to be weak in the face of the Jewish crowd. Earthly rulers are only human, even if they do have the power of life and death over people.
- Jesus made it clear that he had come to save people. God would save the Christians in their persecution.
- God's Holy Spirit was with Jesus in the gospel. The Holy Spirit would be with them in their difficulties to give them the strength to cope.

**B**   *An early Roman Christian*

**Research activity**

Find out where Christians are being persecuted in the world today.

### Activities

1. Why did Christians remain within Judaism at first?
2. What happened to create a separation between those who followed Judaism and the Christians?
3. Why did the Romans persecute the Christians?
4. Give four reasons why persecuted Christians may have felt supported by Luke's Gospel.
5. How would a written gospel help to develop the community of early Christians?

**Summary**

You will now know that the early Christians were persecuted by the Jews and the Romans by the time Luke was written. You will be able to explain that the gospel would give them hope.

### Luke 1:1–4

Introductions like the one that Luke wrote were very common in ancient Greek writings. However, the introduction to Luke's Gospel is unique in the Bible. It is worth comparing it to the introduction to the Acts of the Apostles, which looks back to Luke's Gospel:

> ❝ In my former book, Theophilus, I wrote about all that Jesus began to do and to teach until the day he was taken up to heaven. ❞
>
> **Acts** 1:1

Luke does not name himself in the introduction to the Gospel. He seems to be writing just to an individual, Theophilus, although people have assumed that the Gospel was written for a much wider audience. Luke could not have known that he was writing documents that would much later become part of the New Testament.

> ❝ Many have undertaken to draw up an account of the things that have been fulfilled among us, just as they were handed down to us by those who from the first were eye-witnesses and servants of the word. Therefore, since I myself have carefully investigated everything from the beginning, it seemed good also to me to write an orderly account for you, most excellent Theophilus, so that you may know the certainty of the things you have been taught. ❞
>
> **Luke** 1:1–4

### Theophilus

Theophilus is Greek for 'lover of God'. Nothing is known about Theophilus, but it is clear from the introduction that he had been taught something of the Christian story, and Luke now wants to write him an 'orderly account'. This suggests that the stories about Jesus and the early written material that was circulating were not organised.

Some have suggested that Theophilus was a leading Roman official or perhaps a local official, and he is described as 'most excellent' so must have had some importance. He clearly did not keep the writing to himself.

### 'Many...'

Luke is aware that there are other versions of the story of the life of Jesus. He doesn't say whether he has used them or not – although, as we have seen, scholars believe that he knew the Gospel

**A** The message of Jesus was carried far and wide by the early Christian missionaries

of Mark. Luke would also have known of the many stories that were circulating about Jesus. Although he says that other people 'have done their best to write a report', Luke is clearly trying to make a very accurate version.

Luke was writing around 80 CE, by which time the message of Jesus had already been carried far and wide by the early Christian missionaries. Paul had travelled throughout the Eastern Mediterranean and had got to Rome with the stories of Jesus. Other missionaries had accompanied him and gone on to Greece, North Africa and Asia Minor. According to tradition, the disciple Thomas went as far as India.

### 'By those who saw...'

Luke was writing at a time when the **eyewitnesses** to some of the events he described were still alive and able to share their experiences. This reference would make Luke's readers believe that his writings were reliable and true.

### 'Servants of the word'

Luke was almost certainly with Paul on his travels. Luke was aware that the eyewitnesses were dying out and that it was left to 'servants of the word', who were determined to share the gospel message around the Roman Empire, to keep the message alive.

**B**  *The title page of Luke from the Lindisfarne Gospels*

### 'Certainty'

It is possible that even as early as the end of the 1st century CE people had begun to tell stories that embellished the facts. Some of them began to create new miracle stories, for example, because they were so keen to emphasise Jesus' divinity. As you work through the gospel, you will see Luke is very clear that while Jesus is the Messiah, the Son of God, he is certainly human.

## Jesus teaches in the synagogue

It is not surprising that Jesus, a Jew, would go to the **synagogue** in his home town of **Nazareth**. Luke writes that when Jesus visited synagogues he was praised for his teaching.

> *Jesus returned to Galilee in the power of the Spirit, and news about him spread through the whole countryside. He taught in their synagogues, and everyone praised him.*
>
> *He went to Nazareth, where he had been brought up, and on the Sabbath day he went into the synagogue, as was his custom. And he stood up to read. The scroll of the prophet Isaiah was handed to him. Unrolling it, he found the place where it is written:*
>
> *'The Spirit of the Lord is on me,*
> *because he has anointed me*
> *to preach good news to the poor.*
> *He has sent me to proclaim freedom for the prisoners*
> *and recovery of sight for the blind,*
> *to release the oppressed,*
> *to proclaim the year of the Lord's favour.'*
>
> *Then he rolled up the scroll, gave it back to the attendant and sat down. The eyes of everyone in the synagogue were fastened on him, and he began by saying to them, 'Today this scripture is fulfilled in your hearing.'*
>
> *Luke 4:14–21*

### Objectives

Know and understand what happened when Jesus preached in Nazareth.

Understand Jesus' message about himself in the synagogue.

### Key terms

**Synagogue**: where Jews meet for worship on the Sabbath. Jesus regularly attended the synagogue.

**Nazareth**: the town in Galilee in which Jesus was brought up.

**Anointing**: oil was poured on the head of Israelite kings at their coronation as a sign that they were chosen by God, and it came to have Messianic significance. The Hebrew term Messiah means 'anointed one'.

## The message that Jesus gave

As Jesus read the prophecy, the characteristics of the Messiah and his actions were identified:

- He will be **anointed** by the Spirit of the Lord. (Remember that this is an important theme in Luke and refers to the baptism (Luke 3:22). The Messiah was the Anointed One.)
- He will preach good news to the poor.
- He will proclaim release to captives.
- He will give sight to the blind.
- He will free those who are oppressed. (People who were enslaved to the Romans might have been very attracted by this claim.)
- He will proclaim the year of the Lord.

### The year of the Lord

In the Old Testament there was a teaching that every 49 years in Israel there would be a Jubilee Year, when all debts were released and the land went back to its proper owners. In the Old Testament (Leviticus 25) four things would happen:

- slaves would be freed
- debts would be wiped out
- property would be returned to its original owner
- the land would become very fertile.

People lived in hope of these things happening.

**A** *Interior of a synagogue*

## ■ Isaiah's prophecy

Jesus was sure that Isaiah's prophecy related to him. He had experienced baptism and had a real sense of being called by God after his period alone in the desert, when he was tempted. His words were very clear: 'Today this scripture is fulfilled in your hearing.' Jesus clearly believes that his role is to fulfil this prophecy.

Jesus had been invited to read from the prophets and chose passages from Isaiah. There would be nothing unusual in this. It was normal for the leader of the synagogue to invite people to read. What was unusual was Jesus' interpretation and the reaction of the people in the synagogue. At this point in Jesus' life he was still working alone; he had not yet gathered the disciples together to support him.

**B**   *Nazareth today*

### The synagogue in Jewish life

'Synagogue' is the Greek word for a building that would have existed in many communities. The building would be used as a community centre, meeting house, place of education and place of worship. It would be where the scrolls were kept. The synagogue would be run by the elders in the village and they would invite people to preach there. This incident in Luke is the earliest record that exists of what happened in a synagogue.

**Activity**

**1**   As you work through Luke, make a note each time there is an example of Jesus doing any of the things in the list mentioned in the passage from Isaiah.

**Research activity**

Look up Isaiah 61:1–2. Compare it with what Jesus read. What was Isaiah promising his readers?

**AQA   Examiner's tip**

Remember when you refer to the synagogue in an answer that it is not like a church. The synagogue was a meeting place, not just a place of worship.

**Activities**

**2**   Explain what a synagogue is.

**3**   Why was it important for Jesus to go to the synagogue to begin to share his message?

**4**   What question did those in the synagogue ask about Jesus?

**5**   Jesus clearly felt that it would be difficult to convince the people in Nazareth that he was the Son of God. Why do you think this was?

**6**   How does Jesus show that he believed that he was working with the Holy Spirit (spirit of the Lord)?

**Summary**

You should now know what Jesus preached about in Nazareth and what happened afterwards.

> " *All spoke well of him and were amazed at the gracious words that came from his lips. 'Isn't this Joseph's son?' they asked.*
>
> *Jesus said to them, 'Surely you will quote this proverb to me: "Physician, heal yourself! Do here in your home town what we have heard that you did in Capernaum."*
>
> *'I tell you the truth,' he continued, 'no prophet is accepted in his home town. I assure you that there were many widows in Israel in Elijah's time, when the sky was shut for three and a half years and there was a severe famine throughout the land. Yet Elijah was not sent to any of them, but to a widow in Zarephath in the region of Sidon. And there were many in Israel with leprosy in the time of Elisha the prophet, yet not one of them was cleansed – only Naaman the Syrian.'*
>
> *All the people in the synagogue were furious when they heard this. They got up, drove him out of the town, and took him to the brow of the hill on which the town was built, in order to throw him down the cliff. But he walked right through the crowd and went on his way.* "
>
> *Luke* 4:22–30

### Objectives

Understand the connections between the passage from Isaiah and Jesus as Messiah.

Know and understand the reaction of the people to Jesus' message.

Think about the importance of Jesus' message to Christians today.

### The reaction of the crowd

However inspired by the Holy Spirit Jesus felt, the crowd were not impressed and they turned on him. It was prophesied in the Old Testament that the Messiah was to be rejected, and this happened in the synagogue that day. First, the crowd were questioning whether this was 'Joseph's son', and not someone special.

They also demanded that Jesus perform a miracle as he had in Capernaum. It is worth noting that Luke has not mentioned Capernaum at this point in the text but the crowd clearly knew that Jesus was building a reputation.

Eventually they were so outraged that they were going to throw him down the cliff at the edge of the city. The text tells us that Jesus walked through the crowd. This is a mysterious comment, but indicates Jesus' power.

### Elijah and Elisha

Jesus refers to Elijah and Elisha, two of the great Old Testament prophets. They told people what God demanded of them. This was the key role of the prophets in the Old Testament – to tell people what God wanted. Sometimes they also foretold the future and did miracles.

Jesus refers to two miracles and makes a point that in both cases the people involved with Elijah and Elisha were not Israelites. This is an early sign that Jesus had not just come for the Jewish people. In Elijah's case a widow in Zarephath in Sidon helped him and he brought her son back from the dead. Elisha told Naaman the Syrian how to be cured of leprosy. Both prophets had experienced rejection by the Israelites.

### ∞ links

For more on the baptism of Jesus, see Chapter 3.

**A**   *The work of the Jubilee Debt Campaign*

**Research activity**

The Jubilee Debt Campaign has been established to try to get rid of world poverty. Find out about their work at www.jubileedebtcampaign.org.uk.

## The rejection of Jesus

**Beliefs and teachings**

I tell you the truth…no prophet is accepted in his home town.

*Luke* 4:24

This phrase has become proverbial. Jesus believed that he had come to serve, but was rejected. He may have been angry or upset at the reaction of the crowd, especially as he was well known to them.

Scholars debate whether by 'his home town' Jesus meant Nazareth or Galilee or the whole of Judea. The important thing is that Jesus was rejected in Nazareth, just as the prophets had said that the Messiah would be (Isaiah 53).

**Discussion activity**

Discuss the meaning of the word 'prophet'. How did Jesus show that he was a prophet?

**B**   *Jesus spent time alone in the desert on a number of occasions*

**Activities**

1   What did Jesus say would be different as a result of his work?

2   What did the Jews expect to happen in a Jubilee Year?

3   How might Christians feel rejected today?

**Summary**

You should now understand Jesus' message to the people of Nazareth and their reaction to it.

### The gospel today

If you think about some of the main themes in Luke – women being treated as equal before God, racism, justice, the outcasts and outsiders – and look at a modern newspaper or the news on TV or radio, you will see that many of the same issues are still important. The groups of people concerned are known as marginalised – they do not quite fit into society and live 'on the edge'. Christians today can show concern for them just as Jesus did.

#### Martin Luther King

Dr Martin Luther King worked for Civil Rights in the USA during the 1950s and 1960s. He realised that Jesus' teaching that all were equal in God's eyes meant that the government should be challenged on its racist laws and practices.

In 1955, in Montgomery, Alabama, a black woman, Rosa Parks, was told that she could not sit on a bus while a white person was standing. She refused to give up her seat. Her refusal was followed by a boycott of the buses, and this led to the formation of the Civil Rights Movement. Led by Dr King, the movement, through a series of non-violent demonstrations and marches, challenged the government to change the law.

In 1963 Dr King led a march to Washington DC, where he gave a speech outlining his dream that his children would be judged by the content of their character, not the colour of their skin. He ended his speech with the phrase 'free at last'. This reflects Jesus' teaching in Luke that he had come to proclaim 'freedom for the oppressed'.

**Objectives**

Think about how the gospel has relevance for today.

**links**

For a definition of vocation, see the Glossary, page 141.

**AQA Examiner's tip**

The examples that follow can be used to illustrate an answer to the question of how Luke's Gospel can encourage Christians to try to improve the lives of others today.

**A** Martin Luther King

**B** The site of Dr King's 'I have a dream' speech

## Christian Aid and empowering women

Christian Aid exists to help the world's marginalised people. It works particularly with women, because it has identified that 70 per cent of the world's poor are women. Christian Aid recognises that this is a human rights issue. Like any group of people in poverty these women suffer from poor educational opportunities. They are unlikely to become leaders. If they cannot be leaders, they cannot change their lot.

Christian Aid works in countries where women need support. One woman they have worked with is Suraya Pakzan from Afghanistan. Suraya Pakzan was awarded the Woman of Courage Award in 2008 for her work in helping the women of Afghanistan resist those who wish to deny them the right to education. There is now an organisation in Afghanistan 'The Voice of Women' which is dedicated to ensuring that women have equal opportunities.

**C**   The work of Christian Aid

## Sylvia Wright

Some people, having read the Gospel, feel called to follow Jesus' teaching in other ways. They feel a sense of vocation, a call from God to serve Him. Some choose to become monks or nuns, or to become priests or ministers of religion.

Another person who responded directly to the teaching in the Gospel of Luke is Sylvia Wright. She took the passage of the Rich Young Ruler (Luke 18:18–25) literally. Sylvia Wright sold everything she had and bought a van that she filled with medicines. She bought a one-way ticket to India, where, despite being thought of as a British spy, she has built a hospital and a school.

**D**   Sylvia Wright

## Other groups and charities

There are many others who follow the teaching of the Gospel of Luke and work for a better distribution of world resources. Organisations such as the Society of St Vincent de Paul and CAFOD, the Catholic Fund for Overseas Development, work to improve the lot of those who have the least. They are putting into practice the teachings of Jesus as recorded in Luke.

- The Society of St Vincent de Paul works with underprivileged people in the UK.
- CAFOD is a Charity established by the Bishops of England and Wales to bring aid to Less Economically Developed Countries (LEDCs).

**Extension activity**

Do some web research on the work of Christian Aid, or Sylvia Wright, or the Society of St Vincent de Paul or CAFOD.

www.christian-aid.org.uk
www.sylviawrighttrust.org
www.svp.org.uk
www.svp-ni.org
www.cafod.org.uk

### Activities

1. Why did Dr Martin Luther King feel it was important to work for the rights of black people in the USA?
2. How did Jesus' work reflect his attitude to those who were oppressed and outside society?
3. Christian Aid raises money and works to improve people's lives across the world. How does this fulfil Jesus' teaching?
4. Should Christians lead the world in working for the rights of outsiders?
5. What can an individual Christian do to follow the example of Jesus in working for the rights of those rejected by others?

**Summary**

You should now understand that the Gospel of Luke has meaning for today and that people have changed their whole lives as result of their interpretation of Jesus' teaching.

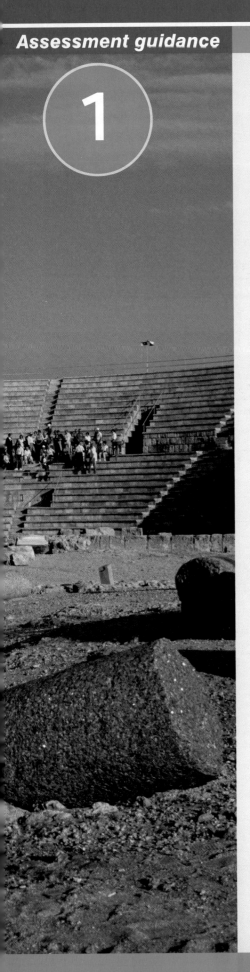

**1**

### Background to St Luke's Gospel – summary

For the examination you should now be able to:

✓ explain what a gospel is and why Luke wrote his Gospel

✓ describe and explain the sources of information that Luke used

✓ consider the information available about Luke as a writer

✓ understand that Luke's Gospel was written for Gentile Christians

✓ understand its nature as good news and salvation history

✓ explain the authority of the Gospel and its relevance for Christians today.

### Sample answer

**1** Write an answer to the following examination question:

'Jesus felt called by God, but people today do not feel they are called by God.' Do you agree? Give reasons for your answer, showing that you have thought about more than one point of view. *(6 marks)*

**2** Read the following sample answer.

> 'Jesus did have a sense of calling from God. This came from his time in the wilderness as he was tempted and is shown by his baptism where the Holy Spirit is said to have come to him. He then went to Nazareth and preached that he was the Messiah. In the synagogue he said that he fulfilled the prophecy of Isaiah that the Messiah would make the blind see and free the oppressed through God's Spirit. It is true that these days people are more interested in what they are paid for a job than just to do it. It is not true though that people do not have a sense of calling. Many people become monks and nuns. Some become priests. Other jobs are also seen as callings such as teaching or nursery nursing or nursing itself. I do not agree with the statement. People do have callings and are not just driven by money and the job.'

**3** With a partner, discuss the sample answer. Do you think there are other things that the student could have included in the answer?

**4** What mark would you give this answer out of 6? Look at the mark scheme in the Introduction on page 7 (AO2). What are the reasons for the mark you have given?

# AQA Examination-style questions

Look at the picture and answer the following questions.

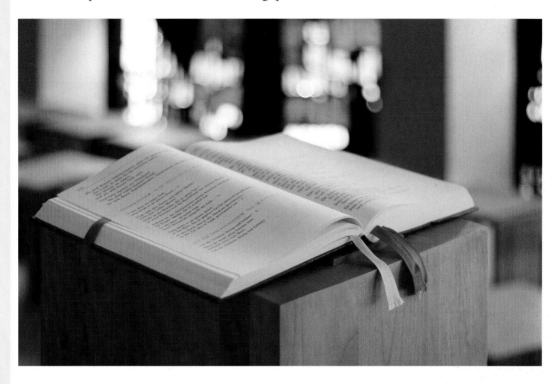

**1**    What does the word 'gospel' mean? *(2 marks)*

**2**    What was the reaction of those in the synagogue in Nazareth when Jesus first preached there? *(3 marks)*

 **Examiner's tip** Look carefully at the number of marks awarded for each question. The number of marks awarded should provide you with a guide as to how many points to make in your answer.

**3**    Explain the importance of the passage from the prophet Isaiah that Jesus read in the synagogue in Nazareth. *(4 marks)*

**4**    'The Gospel of Luke was written too long after Jesus lived to be of value.' Do you agree? Give reasons for your answer. *(3 marks)*

**5**    'Luke shows that Jesus was the Messiah in order to encourage those who have nothing.' Do you agree? Give reasons for your answer, showing that you have thought about more than one point of view. *(6 marks)*

# 2 Salvation

## 2.1 Salvation and the Jewish faith

**Salvation** is a very important concept for religious believers. This was particularly the case with the Jews with whom Jesus lived and worked. Jesus was born and died a Jew. The Jews believed that salvation came from God and that God could intervene in history to change things for the better – to help them or 'save' them. Two events above all others illustrate this belief. The first is the Exodus from Egypt around 1280–1250 BCE, and the second is the period after the Jews were taken to Babylon, known as the Exile in 597–539 BCE.

### The Exodus

Moses was chosen by God at the incident of the Burning Bush (Exodus 3) and told to go to the Egyptian Pharaoh with the demand that the Jews living and working in Egypt should be released. Pharaoh refused to let the people go and then ten plagues followed. The plagues became increasingly severe until, on the night of the first Passover, the angel of death is said to have gone throughout Egypt killing the first born of every family (Exodus 12). The Jewish families survived, provided that they had followed Moses' instructions to mark their doors with the blood of a sacrificed lamb.

Pharaoh at first gave permission for the Jews to leave, but then changed his mind and sent troops after them. As the Jews approached the Red Sea, God parted the waters so that they could escape, but when the Egyptians followed the waters closed, and they were drowned.

The Jewish Festival of the Passover commemorates the saving of the Jewish people from Egypt.

#### The Covenant

The Jews had experienced salvation from God. He had showed that he was powerful and would care for them and in return they were expected to keep the laws of God and live as a holy people. This was an agreement with God (the Covenant): 'I will be your God and you will be my people.' For the Jews, the most important part of the agreement was to keep the Law.

### The Exile

In 597 BCE the Jewish nation was attacked and overwhelmed by Babylonian forces, and the leaders of the Jewish nation were taken to Babylon as prisoners. This period became known as the Exile. This was a desperate time for the Jews who had believed, despite the warnings of prophets, that God would protect them.

**Objectives**

Understand the meaning of salvation.

Know and understand events in Jewish history linked to salvation.

**Key terms**

**Salvation**: saving the soul, deliverance from sin and admission to heaven brought about by Jesus.

**A** A seder plate

A 'saviour', Cyrus, King of Persia, emerged in 539 BCE and ordered that all exiles could return to their land. He also agreed to support the restoration of the Temple in Jerusalem.

## King Cyrus

These verses are taken from Isaiah:

> 66 *The Lord says of Cyrus, 'He is my shepherd and will accomplish all that I please.* 99
>
> *Isaiah 44:28*

> 66 *This is what the LORD says to his anointed, to Cyrus…* 99
>
> *Isaiah 45:1*

Cyrus is described in terms similar to those used to describe Jesus: 'anointed' and a 'shepherd'. These are both terms used of the Messiah. Cyrus is credited with freeing the Jews, and therefore becomes part of God's salvation for them: part of their salvation history. God has intervened to have the Jews released from their exile.

**B** *King Cyrus*

### AQA Examiner's tip

You will not be examined on the Exodus or the Exile, but knowing about them is useful background information.

### Extension activity

During the Second World War the Jews suffered the Holocaust. This was an attempt to wipe out the Jews in Europe. Do some research on this. How does this fit in with their idea that God is their God and they are his people?

## Activities

1. Find out about the Jewish Passover. In it the youngest child asks four questions. What are they?
2. What do the answers teach about the Jewish understanding of salvation?
3. How did the Jews regard Cyrus?
4. Do people today feel that salvation is needed?
5. Is there any evidence that God intervenes in world events today?

### Summary

You should now know ways in which the Jewish people understood salvation and how they believe that God intervenes in history.

## 2.2 Salvation in Jesus' time

### Faith and salvation

In Jewish and Christian understanding there is a link between faith and salvation. As you work through the Gospel of Luke, you will notice that on a number of occasions Jesus says faith has saved a person. It is through faith that the miracles happen and through faith that sins are forgiven. Jesus condemned those who had little faith – including the disciples (Luke 8:25).

The problem for many of Jesus' hearers was that they had the idea that he should be getting rid of the Romans. When he did not do this but appeared to be a peaceful **Messiah**, they rejected him and his message. The early Christians, however, understood that Jesus' salvation was not a warlike thing but a matter of forgiveness from sin and a relationship with God. They also realised that life after death was as aspect of salvation.

### Jewish self-rule

Before the Romans came, the Jews had had a period of self-rule between 167 BCE and 70 BCE. This had left them – particularly in Galilee – with a fervent hope that a Messiah or Saviour would arise and lead them to freedom again. The people were looking for salvation. For them salvation was getting rid of the Romans.

There were a number of rebel leaders at about the time of Jesus whom they hoped would be 'the one'. One of these was Judas the Galilean: he led a rebellion in 6 CE, but it was unsuccessful.

Luke says of John the Baptist, 'The people were waiting expectantly and were all wondering in their hearts if John might possibly be the Christ.' (Luke 3:15)

### The Jewish War 66–74 CE

In 66–74 CE there was a terrible war between Jewish rebels and the Romans. The Jews hoped that in the chaos of the war the Messiah would appear and save them. Despite a number of people claiming to be the Messiah, the Jews lost the war and lost their independence.

Luke would have been aware of this – indeed, he may have been affected by it. He appears to have known that the Temple was destroyed in 70 CE and that many Jewish people were killed.

### Jesus and salvation history

From the beginning, Jesus was recognised by the author of Luke as part of God's plan for the world. In the birth stories, God is seen as intervening in history again.

**Objectives**

Understand what salvation the Jews hoped for in the 1st century CE.

**Key terms**

**Messiah:** the person whom God will send to save humanity, believed by Christians to be Jesus (the Anointed One). Hebrew form of the word Christ.

**AQA** *Examiner's tip*

Remember that the Jewish view of the Messiah was political. The Jews thought he would rid them of the Romans.

During their difficult times under the Romans, Christians were hoping that Jesus would come again, for a second time. But that did not happen. When he was planning to write his Gospel and the Acts of the Apostles, Luke will have been well aware of their disappointment.

It was clear that salvation was not going to be about defeating the Romans. Increasingly, it looked like something linked with life after death.

### Extension activity

Find out the meaning of the word 'parousia'. Why would this have been important to the early Christians, especially during the 66–74 war?

 **A**   *A coin from the time of the Jewish War against Rome*

**B**   *Impression of the temple before it was destroyed*

### Discussion activity

Discuss with another student what links there might be between faith and salvation.

### Activities

1. What did the Jewish people expect the Messiah to do for them?
2. How do we know that they were expecting a Messiah?
3. What type of salvation did Jesus offer?
4. Is salvation something that can only be experienced after death?

### Summary

You should now understand that salvation was something the Jews wanted in Jesus' time and that they expected it to rid them of the Romans. You should also know that this was not Jesus' understanding of the role of the Messiah.

# A birth is announced

> 66 *In the sixth month, God sent the angel Gabriel to Nazareth, a town in Galilee, to a virgin pledged to be married to a man named Joseph, a descendant of David. The virgin's name was Mary. The angel went to her and said, 'Greetings, you who are highly favoured! The Lord is with you.'*
>
> *Mary was greatly troubled at his words and wondered what kind of greeting this might be. But the angel said to her, 'Do not be afraid, Mary, you have found favour with God. You will be with child and give birth to a son, and you are to give him the name Jesus. He will be great and will be called the Son of the Most High. The Lord God will give him the throne of his father David, and he will reign over the house of Jacob for ever; his kingdom will never end.'*
>
> *'How will this be,' Mary asked the angel, 'since I am a virgin?'*
>
> *The angel answered, 'The Holy Spirit will come upon you, and the power of the Most High will overshadow you. So the holy one to be born will be called the Son of God. Even Elizabeth your relative is going to have a child in her old age, and she who was said to be barren is in her sixth month. For nothing is impossible with God.'*
>
> *'I am the Lord's servant,' Mary answered. 'May it be to me as you have said.' Then the angel left her.* 99
>
> **Luke** 1:38

### Objectives

Develop knowledge and understanding of the annunciation.

Recognise the importance of this narrative for an understanding of Jesus.

### Key terms

**Holy Spirit**: the third person of the Holy Trinity who descended like a dove on Jesus at his baptism. Christians believe that the Holy Spirit is present and inspires them.

This passage is important to Luke because it enables him to show very early in the Gospel that Jesus is the Messiah. For Luke, the important person in the story is Mary, who is shown as the servant of the Lord. 'I am the Lord's servant,' said Mary; 'may it be to me as you have said.' (Luke 1:38) Luke's account here emphasises Mary's obedience.

## The announcement

The angel Gabriel visited Mary 'in the sixth month'. This refers to the sixth month of her relative Elizabeth's pregnancy. Elizabeth had had an equally surprising experience. Her husband Zechariah was a priest in the Temple in Jerusalem. He was told that Elizabeth would have a son (Luke 1:5–25), who would be filled by the **Holy Spirit** and would act like Elijah to bring the Israelites back to their faith. Elizabeth and Zechariah's son was John the Baptist.

### Research activity

This is not the first time in the Bible that a birth was predicted. Look up Judges 13:2–7 and read about Samson's mother.

Mary lived in Nazareth, a small town in Galilee. Galilee was in the north, and the people there were looked down upon by those in Jerusalem. The Galileans were regarded as not quite pure Jewish, and the Pharisees were known to question whether anything good could come from Galilee. They were, however, practising Jews and regularly travelled to Jerusalem for the festivals.

Mary was engaged to Joseph. In the 1st century CE this was the first stage in the marriage process. The young woman might well have left her family home and moved in with her husband-to-be. This would not mean that they were 'living together' in the modern meaning of the word, and it is clear from Luke's narrative that Mary and Joseph had not

**A**   *The Annunciation by Botticelli*

had sexual relations. Luke notes that Joseph was a descendant of King David, using this as another piece of evidence of Jesus' messianic nature.

Gabriel appeared to Mary and greeted her. The word angel means 'messenger', and angels were regarded as messengers of God who brought information to those they visited. In the Old Testament angels brought messages (Judges 13:3), caused destruction (2 Samuel 24:16), protected people (Exodus 14:19) and were a sign of the presence of God (Daniel 3:28). Many believe that angels are one of the ways in which God communicated with humans.

Mary was disturbed by what the angel told her as she was not yet married, so having a child would mean she could face disgrace. The angel told Mary not to be afraid. This is the same reassurance that the shepherds are also given later.

## Mary's question

**B**   *Artistic depiction of an angel*

> 66 *Mary said to the angel, 'How will this be, since I am a virgin?'* 99
> *Luke* 1:34

Mary asks the obvious question. It remains a question for some believers today: was Mary a 'virgin'? The debate centres around Isaiah 7:14. In this passage the prophet announces 'a young woman who is pregnant will have a son and will name him "Immanuel"'. The Hebrew word in the passage literally means 'young woman' but is translated as 'virgin'. The Greek word is *parthenos*, which also means a young woman. Some people therefore think that the idea of a virgin birth resulted from an interpretation of this passage from Isaiah.

## Activities

1   Why was Mary 'troubled' by the angel's visit?
2   What is the importance of the name 'Jesus'?
3   In what way does the annunciation identify Jesus as the Messiah?
4   How does Mary set an example for Christians today?
5   'The annunciation proves that Jesus is the Messiah.' Do you agree? Give reasons for your answer.

## Summary

You should now know and understand what happened at the annunciation and its importance in understanding that Jesus is Messiah.

# The importance of the birth announcement

## ■ Names of the baby

Luke wanted to make certain that readers of the narrative of the annunciation were in no doubt that the baby Mary was to give birth to was the Messiah.

### Jesus

Jesus is the Greek version of the Hebrew name 'Joshua'. This was the name of many men at the time, and means Yahweh [God] saves. Luke clearly expected that his readers would understand the meaning of the name, because he does not go into any more detail about its meaning.

If you look at Matthew's version of the story, you will see that he adds the phrase 'because he will save the people from their sins' (Matthew 1:21). The early Christians would have understood that Jesus had been born to save them. This belief would have been important to them because when many died under persecution they would face it with the faith that they were saved.

### Son of the Most High

'Most High' is a title for God. It is used several times in the writings of Luke. Mark uses it once (5:7), and it is used many times in the Old Testament. By the use of this phrase, Jesus is described very clearly as God's son.

**Key terms**

**Son of God:** a title used for Jesus. The second person of the Trinity; denotes the special relationship between Jesus and God. Christians believe that before his birth as a human being, Jesus always existed as God the Son. Also means a righteous man.

**A**   *Jesus the Messiah is depicted in a 6th-century mosaic from Ravenna*

## The throne of his father David

This is not really a title of Jesus as such but Luke was drawing attention to Joseph's ancestry. Jesus was called 'Son of David' elsewhere in the gospel and this almost certainly led to the belief that Jesus was a political Messiah. It may even have motivated Judas in his actions in handing Jesus over to the authorities (see pages 16–17).

At this time the Jews were hoping for a Messiah who would be able to establish God's rule and be king. However, Jesus never claimed to be a king.

## Son of God

It is a mark of the importance that Luke places on establishing Jesus' authority that he uses the term '**Son of God**'.

In Psalm 2:7 there is a reference to the Messiah being the Son of God: 'You are my Son; today I have become your father.' Yet the phrase 'Son of God' is not used only of Jesus. In the Old Testament it refers sometimes to angels, to the nation of Israel, to King David and to some other individuals.

However, the message Luke is trying to give is that Jesus is the Messiah, and as he is writing for believers he has no hesitation in using the title Son of God. In Luke Jesus refers to God as 'Abba', meaning 'father', which shows that he later believed that he was the Son of God. In the baptism and the transfiguration Jesus is referred to by God as 'my son'.

'Son of God' was at once the most important and the most dangerous title applied to Jesus. Anyone claiming to be the Son of God committed blasphemy which is claiming to be equal with God or using his name in a disrespectful way. At the trial before the Council he was asked directly if he was the Son of God. Jesus replied very carefully: 'You are right in saying I am' (Luke 22:70). Saying this led to his conviction.

**B**   *Jesus 'Son of God'*

### Beliefs and teachings

I will proclaim the decree of the Lord:

> He said to me, 'You are my Son today I have become your Father.
> Ask of me, and I will make the nations your inheritance, the ends of the earth your possession.'

*Psalms* 2:7-8

### Activities

1. Why is the name of Jesus important?
2. Jesus is described as 'Son of the Most High'. What does this mean?
3. Explain the meaning of the word 'annunciation'.
4. Why was using the phrase 'Son of God' dangerous?

### Summary

You should now know and understand the titles of Jesus used in the narrative of the annunciation.

### Bethlehem

Everyone who has celebrated Christmas will be familiar with the scene. Christmas cards picture a stable with Mary and Joseph, and a baby in a manger. Very often there are angels, shepherds and animals. The place was Bethlehem. Each Christmas, despite the political pressures that exist in Bethlehem now, people from around the world go to worship in the church built on the traditional site of the stable.

Bethlehem is a town about eight miles from Jerusalem. It was the place where King David was born, and where in about 1000 BCE he was chosen by Samuel the Prophet to become King of Israel. He was anointed King, and Bethlehem was thereafter known as the City of David.

That a ruler would come from Bethlehem had been predicted by the prophet Micah in the 8th century BCE. Luke does not refer to this directly, but he does describe how **Jesus** was descended from David (Luke 4:32). It was important that Jesus was born in Bethlehem, because it linked him back to King David. This meant he could be called Son of David and be seen as the Messiah.

### The birth of Jesus

> *In those days Caesar Augustus issued a decree that a census should be taken of the entire Roman world. (This was the first census that took place while Quirinius was governor of Syria.) And everyone went to his own town to register. So Joseph also went up from the town of Nazareth in Galilee to Judea, to Bethlehem the town of David, because he belonged to the house and line of David. He went there to register with Mary, who was pledged to be married to him and was expecting a child. While they were there, the time came for the baby to be born, and she gave birth to her firstborn, a son. She wrapped him in cloths and placed him in a manger, because there was no room for them in the inn.*
>
> *Luke* 2:1–7

Joseph and Mary were in Bethlehem, we are told, because a census had been called by the Governor Quirinius. There was a census by Quirinius in 6 CE, but this is too late for it to be linked to Jesus' birth. However, the author of Luke is very certain that Mary and Joseph were in Bethlehem, Joseph's home town, and that the baby was born there. Luke may have been referring to some administrative organisation that Quirinius was making.

#### The date of Jesus' birth

No one knows the exact date when Jesus was born, but 25 December is the traditional date celebrated by Christians in the West. However, if Jesus was actually born on that day of the year, it is very unlikely that the shepherds would have been in the fields. The animals would by this time have been brought down into the town for warmth and safety during the winter.

**A** *Bethlehem today*

**Objectives**

Study the account of the birth of Jesus.

Consider the importance of this account for an understanding of the message of the Gospel.

Evaluate the importance of this narrative in understanding the message of salvation.

**Key terms**

**Jesus**: 1st-century Jewish teacher and holyman, believed by Christians to be the Son of God.

**AQA Examiner's tip**

The important thing to understand here is that the gospel writer, through these narratives, was supporting the belief that Jesus was the Messiah. Therefore being born in Bethlehem was an important factor.

**B**   *The Church of the Nativity in Bethlehem*

## Where were Mary and Joseph staying?

There are references in the Christmas tradition to a stable. Some English translations use the term 'inn' (RSV, NIV, GNB). The word used means 'living space' or 'lodging', and it has been suggested that Mary and Joseph were staying in the lower half of a house in which the people lived upstairs. The lower part of the house was where the animals were kept, and so the manger would have been there.

Mary acted just as any other mother would in wrapping her baby in cloths. She then used the manger as a makeshift cot. The manger is important because it is a sign to the shepherds and will indicate that they have found the correct baby. In religious terms, the idea that the new Messiah is laid in a place where animals eat could have the symbolic meaning that the Messiah would 'feed' the people.

### Activities

1. Find out why Orthodox Christians celebrate Christmas Day on 6 January.
2. Does it matter whether Luke was correct in referring to the census in the stories of Jesus' birth?
3. What is the importance of the phrase 'Town of David?'
4. Why is a manger important in the story?

### Research activity

There is a great deal of debate over Jesus' actual date of birth. Use the internet to find some of the arguments about the use of 25 December, which was originally a Roman festival.

### Summary

You should now understand how the birth stories point to Jesus being the Messiah. You should be able to evaluate how important these stories are for an understanding of the message of salvation.

### The shepherds

> *There were shepherds living out in the fields near by, keeping watch over their flocks at night. An angel of the Lord appeared to them, and the glory of the Lord shone around them, and they were terrified. But the angel said to them, 'Do not be afraid. I bring you good news of great joy that will be for all the people. Today in the town of David a Saviour has been born to you; he is Christ the Lord. This will be a sign to you: You will find a baby wrapped in cloths and lying in a manger.'*
>
> *Suddenly a great company of the heavenly host appeared with the angel, praising God and saying,*
> *'Glory to God in the highest,*
> *and on earth peace to men on whom his favour rests.'*
>
> *When the angels had left them and gone into heaven, the shepherds said to one another, 'Let's go to Bethlehem and see this thing that has happened, which the Lord has told us about.'*
>
> *So they hurried off and found Mary and Joseph, and the baby, who was lying in the manger. When they had seen him, they spread the word concerning what had been told them about this child, and all who heard it were amazed at what the shepherds said to them. But Mary treasured up all these things and pondered them in her heart. The shepherds returned, glorifying and praising God for all the things they had heard and seen, which were just as they had been told.*
>
> *Luke 2:8–20*

Shepherds were very important in 1st-century Palestine because the animals they kept provided food and wool, but they would have been poor. The shepherds were hired workmen; few of them would have owned the sheep they were looking after. They were responsible for the safety and welfare of their flock and they took great care of them.

Because shepherds demonstrated care for their flock, God is often described as a shepherd in the Old Testament, and Jesus is described as the Good Shepherd in the New Testament. It was to shepherds that the first revelation of the Messiah was made.

### The angel's message

The angel is said to have appeared to the shepherds and told them: 'Do not be afraid! I bring you good news.' Notice that they are told not to be afraid, and Mary had been told exactly the same thing in the annunciation. The pattern is the same: an angelic visit; the fear of those visited; the instruction not to be afraid; and the message that good news will bring excitement and joy. The angel is promising the shepherds that there will be good news for everyone.

The shepherds were told to go and find a baby in a manger, wrapped in cloths, in the city of David. They were told that the baby was the

**A** *Shepherds were very important in 1st-century Palestine*

Saviour and Christ the Lord. These are both messianic titles. The reaction of the shepherds was to be 'terrified'. More angels appeared and they sang, 'Glory to God in the highest, and on earth peace to men on whom his favour rests.' Peace was something that was important in Israel as a sign of God's presence: peace came from God. Peace was far more than the absence of conflict or war; it meant harmony, wellbeing – a peaceful state of mind in which people could flourish.

The shepherds then visited the baby and we are told that they returned glorifying and praising God for all the things they had heard and seen, which were just as they had been told. Notice the difference in their feelings; they were no longer terrified. They were full of wonder, joy and expectation.

## The salvation theme

The birth stories emphasise Luke's themes that God intervenes in history, and that ordinary, poor people can be brought into contact with God to gain a sense of salvation. Geza Vermes, a Jewish writer, describes it in this way: 'Luke's low key birth narrative depicts a simple and unspectacular rural event' (*The Nativity*, page 103). Mary and Joseph were poor – or at least it is not unreasonable to assume that they were. The shepherds were also poor. Yet it is to these people that the birth of the Messiah was entrusted and announced.

### Extension activity

Find out how Jewish people view peace by looking up the meaning of the word 'shalom'.

**B** *William Blake's painting of the shepherds*

### Activities

1. Why do you think the shepherds were the first people that the birth was announced to?
2. What is the importance of the angels in this story?
3. Make a list in your notebook of all the ways in which Luke emphasises in this narrative that Jesus is the Messiah.
4. How do the birth narratives show that God is intervening in history?
5. Do you agree with Geza Vermes that the birth of Jesus was a 'low key' event?

### Summary

You should now know the story of the shepherds and understand its importance for the message of the gospel and its message of salvation.

# Jesus is presented in the Temple

## The meeting with Simeon

> When the time of their purification according to the Law of Moses had been completed, Joseph and Mary took him to Jerusalem to present him to the Lord (as it is written in the Law of the Lord, 'Every firstborn male is to be consecrated to the Lord'), and to offer a sacrifice in keeping with what is said in the Law of the Lord: 'a pair of doves or two young pigeons'.
>
> Now there was a man in Jerusalem called Simeon, who was righteous and devout. He was waiting for the consolation of Israel, and the Holy Spirit was upon him. It had been revealed to him by the Holy Spirit that he would not die before he had seen the Lord's Christ. Moved by the Spirit, he went into the temple courts. When the parents brought in the child Jesus to do for him what the custom of the Law required, Simeon took him in his arms and praised God, saying.
>
> 'Sovereign Lord, as you have promised,
> you now dismiss your servant in peace.
> For my eyes have seen your salvation,
> which you have prepared in the sight of all people,
> a light for revelation to the Gentiles
> and for glory to your people Israel.'
>
> The child's father and mother marvelled at what was said about him. Then Simeon blessed them and said to Mary, his mother: 'This child is destined to cause the falling and rising of many in Israel, and to be a sign that will be spoken against, so that the thoughts of many hearts will be revealed. And a sword will pierce your own soul too.'

*Luke* 2:22–35

### Objectives

Study the incidents surrounding Jesus being taken to the Temple.

Consider the importance of the words of Simeon.

### Key terms

**The Temple**: the most holy place of the Jews, built in Jerusalem and the centre of their worship. It was destroyed by the Romans in 70 CE.

**A** *An artist's impression of Christ*

Simeon had been waiting for the Messiah to appear. He entered **the Temple** because hc felt moved by the Holy Spirit. As soon as he saw Mary, Joseph and the child, he took the child into his arms. Just by holding Jesus, Simeon was able to recognise that this was a special baby.

Simeon does not appear anywhere else in the narratives of Jesus but plays an important part in recognising him as the Messiah. His words about Jesus are now used in many Christian services each Sunday.

### Who was Simeon?

Simeon is described as 'righteous and devout', and as a person who possessed the Holy Spirit. He was clearly very respected. Attempts have been made to identify him as a priest or someone important in the Temple, but there is no evidence for this.

**B** *Plan of the Jerusalem Temple in the time of Jesus*

## Luke's themes

There are some themes in this passage that you will find throughout Luke's Gospel:

- **Peace:** The Messiah will bring peace and wellbeing for all.
- **Salvation:** For some this means getting rid of the Romans; for others it means being close to God.
- **Israel:** It is important that the Messiah has come for Israel and for the Jews.
- **Gentiles:** Luke wants to emphasise that the Messiah has come to save not just the Jews but the whole world.

Simeon also gives a prediction of the death of Jesus, and possibly a reference to the crucifixion and resurrection. When he addresses Mary, he predicts her sorrow at the death of Jesus.

## Mary in Jerusalem

Mary is central to this story. It was the Jewish tradition for a mother to be purified after giving birth, and Mary was able to go to the Temple for this. She would have gone to the Court of the Women in Temple at Jerusalem. Her offering ensured that she was ritually clean following childbirth. Mary sacrificed a pair of doves or pigeons, which would have been the sacrifice of a poor person.

### Extension activity

Hymns are important in the Bible. There have already been two in Luke. Look at these hymns, The Magnificat (Luke 1:46–55) and the Song of Zechariah (Luke 1:67–79). Make a list of the references to God intervening in history and the ideas of being saved.

### AQA Examiner's tip

Be able to answer a question that refers to different people recognising Jesus as the Messiah.

### Activities

1. Why did Mary go to Jerusalem?
2. What did she do when she got there?
3. Why do you think Joseph is hardly mentioned?
4. What can Christians learn from Simeon's words to Mary?
5. In what ways does the Presentation in the Temple emphasise the idea that Jesus was going to bring salvation?

### Summary

You should now be able to describe the meeting with Simeon and recognise the importance of his words.

# The healing of Jairus' daughter

## Salvation and faith

Salvation has been seen so far as an idea of freedom and a sense of peace. In this **miracle** and that of the woman with a haemorrhage (pages 50–51), salvation means something very personal to the people concerned. These two stories are also found in the gospels of Mark and Matthew, and all versions are very similar.

## A father's faith

> A man named Jairus, a ruler of the synagogue, came and fell at Jesus' feet, pleading with him to come to his house because his only daughter, a girl of about twelve, was dying.
>
> …
>
> While Jesus was still speaking, someone came from the house of Jairus, the synagogue ruler. 'Your daughter is dead,' he said. 'Don't bother the teacher any more.'
>
> Hearing this, Jesus said to Jairus, 'Don't be afraid; just believe, and she will be healed.'
>
> When he arrived at the house of Jairus, he did not let anyone go in with him except Peter, John and James, and the child's father and mother. Meanwhile, all the people were wailing and mourning for her. 'Stop wailing,' Jesus said. 'She is not dead but asleep.'
>
> They laughed at him, knowing that she was dead. But he took her by the hand and said, 'My child, get up!' Her spirit returned, and at once she stood up. Then Jesus told them to give her something to eat. Her parents were astonished, but he ordered them not to tell anyone what had happened
>
> *Luke* 8:40–42, 49–56

The faith in this miracle is the father's, on behalf of his very sick daughter. Jairus was the ruler of the synagogue and would have been in charge of arrangements for all the different uses of the synagogue. It must have taken him a lot of courage to approach Jesus, given his important position in the community.

The most important things to note in this miracle are:

- The crowd were pleased to see Jesus return from across the lake. This is a reaction that is quite common in the early part of the gospel. Jesus was clearly quite popular in the beginning.

- Jesus was approached by Jairus, who was totally convinced that his 12-year-old daughter was dying and was sure that Jesus could heal her. His faith was unquestioning.

- Despite the fact that people came from Jairus' house to tell him that his daughter was dead, Jesus told him not to be afraid but to have faith.

**Objectives**

Know and understand a healing miracle of Jesus.

Understand the link between faith and salvation.

**Key terms**

**Miracle**: an event that lies beyond normal human knowledge and understanding. It is an unexpected event with religious significance.

- Jesus took only Peter, John and James into the house with him. This seems to be the beginning of an inner circle of disciples.
- The people outside the house laughed at Jesus when he said that the girl was not dead, but only asleep.
- Jesus' command to the girl had an instant effect: she got up. Jesus told the people to give her something to eat. This is the correct procedure for someone who has been in a diabetic coma.
- The parents were astonished.
- Jesus then told them not to tell anyone about what had happened.

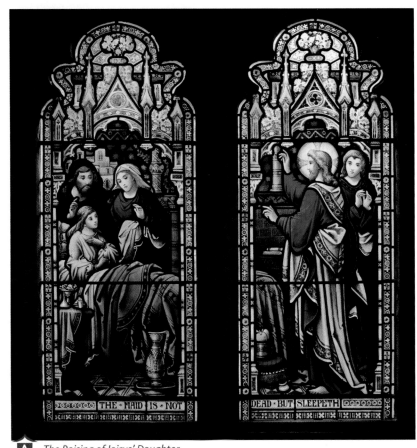

**A**   *The Raising of Jairus' Daughter*

### The miracle and afterwards

This miracle raises real problems for people today. How could Jesus have known that she was not dead? Or perhaps she was dead, and he was so sure of his powers from God that, even so, he knew that he could raise her.

Another question that can be asked is how the parents could possibly keep this event quiet. One explanation for the instruction of Jesus to the family to tell no one is that it is a comment taken from the Gospel of Mark. Mark tried to show Jesus as keeping his messianic claims secret.

**Activities**

1. Why would it have been difficult for Jairus to approach Jesus?
2. How did Jairus demonstrate faith in Jesus?
3. Why do you think the crowd reacted as they did when Jesus said the girl was not dead?
4. Imagine that you are that girl, some years later. Tell the story the way she might tell it to others.
5. Does the miracle lose any of its value if the girl was only in a coma? Say why it does or does not.

**Summary**

You should now know and understand the healing Jairus' daughter and understand the link between faith and salvation.

### The woman's faith

> As Jesus was on his way, the crowds almost crushed him. And a woman was there who had been subject to bleeding for twelve years, but no one could heal her. She came up behind him and touched the edge of his cloak, and immediately her bleeding stopped.
>
> 'Who touched me?' Jesus asked.
>
> When they all denied it, Peter said, 'Master, the people are crowding and pressing against you.'
>
> But Jesus said, 'Someone touched me; I know that power has gone out from me.'
>
> Then the woman, seeing that she could not go unnoticed, came trembling and fell at his feet. In the presence of all the people, she told why she had touched him and how she had been instantly healed. Then he said to her, 'Daughter, your faith has healed you. Go in peace.'
>
> Luke 8:43–48

This narrative is perhaps an even more dramatic example of faith leading to salvation than the healing of Jairus' daughter. These are the key moments:

- The woman has had bleeding for 12 years. The author emphasises that this was a condition that was well established, and not a sudden illness that just cured itself.
- She had spent all that she had on doctors, and they had not succeeded in curing her.
- The crowd were very keen to be with Jesus and trying to get close to him so that they could hear what he said.
- All the woman had to do was touch his cloak, and she was cured instantly – just as Jairus' daughter was cured instantly.
- Jesus felt the power go out of him. This phrase suggests that the act of a person with faith seemed to affect Jesus in some way.
- The disciples did not understand this, and merely blamed the crowd for touching Jesus. They could not believe, with such a crowd, that Jesus would notice someone touching him.
- The woman was frightened when she approached Jesus to tell him that it was she who had touched him.
- Jesus' words to her were: 'Daughter, your faith has healed you. Go in peace.'

**Objectives**

Know and understand a healing miracle of Jesus.

Understand the link between faith and salvation.

**Beliefs and teachings**

Jewish people believed that sin led to suffering. Jesus healed by forgiving sin on some occasions.

**AQA Examiner's tip**

Notice that Jesus gave the woman peace. This is another example of Jesus giving peace – the peaceful Messiah.

**Research activity**

Read the story of Jesus healing ten lepers (Luke 17:11–19). What does this tell you about Jesus' attitude to outcasts and Samaritans.

## Women and outcasts

This story is a good example of Jesus' attitude towards women and outcasts. Under Jewish Law, the woman with a **haemorrhage** would have been regarded as unclean. No one would have wanted to be touched by her, or to touch her. Jesus could have been angry at her for touching him, but instead he treated her in an extremely caring way. He even called her 'daughter'.

In this miracle and that of Jairus' daughter, Jesus demonstrated the importance of salvation. Not only did Jesus cure the two people, but he demonstrated his willingness to risk being regarded as unclean. He touched what was apparently a dead body, and a woman regarded as unclean touched him. These are two of the examples we find in Luke of Jesus' willingness to challenge and reverse existing attitudes to outcast groups.

## Faith and healing

The traditional Jewish view was that sin led to illness. In this case we do not know whether the woman felt the weight of sin but it is clear that she had faith in Jesus' power to cure her of her illness. Christians today believe that there is a link between faith and healing.

**Key terms**

**Haemorrhage:** severe loss of blood.

**Extension activity**

Find out about the work of Father Damien of Molokai. He worked with lepers at a time when leprosy could not be cured easily, if at all.

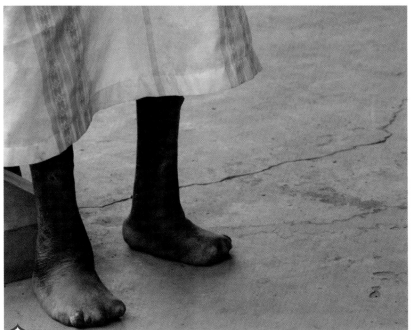

A  Leprosy

B  Father Damien of Molokai

**Activities**

1  Was Jesus wrong to be prepared to be considered ritually unclean?

2  Make a note of the different reactions to Jesus in this story.

3  What do you think is the link between faith and healing in this story and in that of the healing of Jairus' daughter?

4  Which groups in society may currently be considered to be outcasts?

5  How should they be treated by Christians?

**Summary**

You should now understand the link between faith and salvation illustrated through this miracle of Jesus.

### Jesus at the Pharisee's house

> One of the Pharisees invited Jesus to have dinner with him, so he went to the Pharisee's house and reclined at the table. When a woman who had lived a sinful life in that town learned that Jesus was eating at the Pharisee's house, she brought an alabaster jar of perfume, and as she stood behind him at his feet weeping, she began to wet his feet with her tears. Then she wiped them with her hair, kissed them and poured perfume on them.
>
> When the Pharisee who had invited him saw this, he said to himself, 'If this man were a prophet, he would know who is touching him and what kind of woman she is – that she is a sinner.'
>
> Jesus answered him, 'Simon, I have something to tell you.'
>
> 'Tell me, teacher,' he said.
>
> 'Two men owed money to a certain money-lender. One owed him five hundred denarii, and the other fifty. Neither of them had the money to pay him back, so he cancelled the debts of both. Now which of them will love him more?'
>
> Simon replied, 'I suppose the one who had the bigger debt cancelled.'
>
> 'You have judged correctly,' Jesus said.
>
> Then he turned towards the woman and said to Simon, 'Do you see this woman? I came into your house. You did not give me any water for my feet, but she wet my feet with her tears and wiped them with her hair. You did not give me a kiss, but this woman, from the time I entered, has not stopped kissing my feet. You did not put oil on my head, but she has poured perfume on my feet. Therefore, I tell you, her many sins have been forgiven – for she loved much. But he who has been forgiven little loves little.'
>
> Then Jesus said to her, 'Your sins are forgiven.'
>
> The other guests began to say among themselves, 'Who is this who even forgives sins?'
>
> Jesus said to the woman, 'Your faith has saved you; go in peace.'
>
> *Luke* 7:36–50

**Objectives**

Study this incident in Jesus' life.

Examine Jesus' attitude to those who were regarded as outsiders.

Understand how Jesus gave salvation to individuals.

**Key terms**

**Parables**: stories told by Jesus that have spiritual meanings.

## ⦾links

This passage is also in Mark 14:3–9. It is set at a different time in Jesus' life and Simon is said to have lived in Bethany. For Mark the event is seen as a foreshadowing of Jesus' death.

The meal was interrupted by the appearance of an unusual guest. That someone should appear at a meal while the guests were eating was not uncommon: it was who she was and what she did that makes the event unusual.

Jesus did not mind that it was a woman, a prostitute, who was touching his feet and he made this quite clear to the crowd. The crowd were negative, as they could so often be when Jesus associated himself with outcasts. Nevertheless, Jesus gave the woman inner peace by forgiving her sins, and we are told that she left in peace.

**A** *The woman used perfume to anoint Jesus' feet*

Jesus' **parable** about the two men who owed money to the money-lender is discussed in detail on pages 54–55.

### The woman's actions

The woman used perfume to anoint Jesus' feet. Her tears fell on his feet and she used her hair as a towel. The woman demonstrated her respect for Jesus in this amazing way. She recognised him as someone who could bring her peace.

### The guests' reaction

The guests were initially surprised. They questioned whether Jesus was really a prophet – he should have recognised that this woman was a sinner. They knew her and her reputation.

After Jesus had said to the woman that her sins were forgiven, the people discussed things amongst themselves. They asked who Jesus was, that he could forgive sins. They would have been outraged at this apparent blasphemy.

### Simon the poor host

Simon had failed to do the traditional things that a good host should do:

- Water had not been poured on Jesus' feet as it should be for a guest.
- Simon did not greet Jesus with a kiss of welcome.
- Simon had not offered Jesus the opportunity to use perfume or anoint him with oil.

Yet the woman had done all these things. Jesus challenged Simon, and pointed out bluntly how he had failed as a host.

> **AQA** *Examiner's tip*
>
> Remember that anointing was a mark of the Messiah. One of the titles of the Messiah in the Old Testament was 'the anointed one' (see page 26).

> *Discussion activity*
>
> What issues about the place of women in Christian tradition does this story raise?

> **Activities**
>
> 1. What should Simon have done as a good host?
> 2. Why were the guests shocked by Jesus' attitude towards the woman?
> 3. What might the actions of the woman reveal about who Jesus was?
> 4. How did the woman show that Simon had failed to do the traditional things that a good host should do?
> 5. What can be learned from this incident about the love of God?

> **Summary**
>
> You should now know and understand an incident when Jesus brought the message of peace and forgiveness to a woman who was an outsider.

The Parable of the Two Debtors

## Debt and forgiveness

> 'Simon, I have something to tell you.'
>
> 'Tell me, teacher,' he said.
>
> 'Two men owed money to a certain money-lender. One owed him five hundred denarii, and the other fifty. Neither of them had the money to pay him back, so he cancelled the debts of both. Now which of them will love him more?'
>
> Simon replied, 'I suppose the one who had the bigger debt cancelled.'
>
> 'You have judged correctly,' Jesus said.
>
> Luke 7:41–43

Jesus told parables to challenge his hearers and to make them question their own actions and attitudes. The parables were always about everyday matters. People would recognise the situations. Jesus was able to use these everyday situations to teach people about God. In this parable one of the debtors owed the money-lender 500 denarii and the other 50 denarii. One denarius was a day's wages for a labourer. Neither of the men were able to pay, but the money-lender released them from their debt.

This parable can be seen as an allegory where the characters all have another meaning:

**A** *Meanings of characters*

| The money-lender | God |
| --- | --- |
| The debtor who owed 500 denarii | The sinful woman |
| The debtor who owed 50 denarii | Simon |

## The challenge to Simon

When Jesus asked Simon who would love the money-lender more, Simon's answer was that it would be the one who owed the most. This shows how Jesus was able to get his hearers to agree with his message. Jesus appears to have ignored Simon's use of 'I suppose', which might have shown his reluctance to give this answer.

Simon was clearly like the second debtor, but he did not recognise his need for salvation. The woman, who was like the first debtor, did. She was rewarded, as Jesus forgave her sins.

### Research activity

Find out about the work of christians against poverty.
See www.capuk.org

---

**Objectives**

Learn about Jesus' parable.

Understand what it teaches about forgiveness.

**Key terms**

**Kingdom of God:** wherever God is honoured as king and his authority accepted. Jesus taught about the Kingdom of God both on earth and in heaven. The rule of God.

**AQA Examiner's tip**

Learn this parable as an example of forgiveness.

🔗 **links**

For more on the idea of forgiving debts, see the activity on page 29.

🔗 **links**

See the Glossary, on page 140, for a definition of debtor.

**B**  *Jesus and the sinful woman at Simon the Pharisee's house*

## Jesus' care for outcasts

Jesus was willing to work with the outcasts and outsiders in society – in this case, it was a woman with a poor reputation.

Jesus emerges in the gospels as someone who challenges anyone who is sure of themselves and their salvation. The **Kingdom of God** that Jesus is bringing will change the normal order of life.

Jesus' message is that the Kingdom of God is open to all, but that people will need to change their attitudes if they are to be accepted into it.

### ∞ links

For more on Jesus working with women and outcasts, see pages 102–103.

### Discussion activity

Discuss whether this parable could apply to the early Christians who were not Jewish (Gentiles).

### Activities

1  The parable challenged Simon – how did it do this?
2  What does the parable teach about God's forgiveness?
3  What is an allegory?
4  What could the incident of the sinful woman and Jesus' parable mean for Christians today?

### Summary

You should now understand the Parable of the Two Debtors, and how it illustrates that God's forgiveness is without limit.

## Salvation – summary

For the examination you should now be able to:

✓ explain the word 'salvation'

✓ explain the importance of the birth stories of Jesus as salvation history

✓ understand what the incident of the rejection at Nazareth showed about who Jesus was

✓ give examples of miracles in which Jesus demonstrated a link between faith and salvation

✓ outline links between faith and salvation

✓ understand Luke's portrayal of Jesus' work of salvation for all, including outcasts and women, and its significance for Christians today.

### Sample answer

1 Write an answer to the following examination question:

'The birth stories in Luke are all that is needed to prove that Jesus is the Messiah.' Do you agree? Give reasons for your answer, showing that you have thought about more than one point of view. *(6 marks)*

2 Read the following sample answer.

'In the birth stories Luke makes it clear that Jesus is the Messiah. Mary is visited by the angel Gabriel and he tells her that she is to have a baby and that he will be God's son. Mary is told that the baby will be born by the work of the Holy Spirit. She was a virgin at the time. Later the angels went to the shepherds and told them to visit Jesus in Bethlehem where they would find him in a manger in cloths. Bethlehem was the city of David and Joseph came from there. The Messiah was to be the Son of David the king. I do not think that the birth stories are the only important thing. As Jesus worked he was able to forgive people's sins and to cure them of their illnesses. This gave them peace. Peace was something the Messiah gave. So in conclusion I think that the birth stories are part of Jesus being the Messiah but there are other stories which show it as well.'

3 With a partner, discuss the sample answer. Do you think that there are other things that the student could have included in the answer?

4 What mark would you give the answer out of 6? Look at the mark scheme in the Introduction on page 7 (AO2). What are the reasons for the mark you have given?

# AQA Examination-style questions

**1**      Describe the annunciation to Mary.      *(5 marks)*

**AQA Examiner's tip**    This needs to be 8–10 lines long. It is a text recall question.

**2**      Why was Mary 'troubled' when she heard the message that she was to have a son?      *(3 marks)*

**AQA Examiner's tip**    You need to give three reasons, or two with explanation.

**3**      **(i)**    In which town was Jesus born?      *(1 mark)*
           **(ii)**   Why was it important that he was born there?      *(2 marks)*

**AQA Examiner's tip**    For part (ii) you need to give two reasons.

**4**      What does the Presentation of Jesus in the Temple show about Jesus' later claim to be the Messiah?      *(4 marks)*

**AQA Examiner's tip**    Show the connections between the main points in Simeon's words and the later activities or teaching of Jesus.

**5**      'Jesus healed people who had faith.' Do you agree with this statement?
Give reasons for your answer.      *(3 marks)*

**AQA Examiner's tip**    This is not asking for two viewpoints – it is a straightforward question.

**6**      Describe in detail **either** the healing of Jairus' daughter **or** the healing of the woman with a haemorrhage.      *(6 marks)*

**AQA Examiner's tip**    In this question you need to be very clear and should not describe both stories. Your account should be detailed, and include what was said and what was done.

**7**      'Without faith there can be no healing.' Do you agree? Give reasons for your answer, showing that you have thought about more than one point of view. Refer to Christian teaching in your answer.      *(6 marks)*

**AQA Examiner's tip**    The key here is to give a view on the statement and reasons for that view. Then give examples of cures that were linked to faith. You should refer to two or three miracles of Jesus to show that you have a full knowledge of the text. Also look at alternatives: drugs in modern medicine work whether you are aware of it or not.

**8**      How does Luke show that Jesus was sent for the salvation of all people?      *(6 marks)*

**AQA Examiner's tip**    In this answer you should give examples of Jesus working with people who were different in terms of their social standing.

## 3.1    The titles of Jesus

### ■ Titles and authority

In the Gospel of Luke, Jesus' authority comes from the titles that were used of him. Sometimes he used the titles himself, but at other times the disciples and people he met used the titles. In each case Jesus is being described as the Messiah.

### The Christ

This title comes from the Greek 'christos', which in turn comes from the Hebrew 'mashiach'. It means 'the Anointed One'. In using this title, Luke refers back to the Old Testament and the idea that the Messiah is the person chosen by God to save Israel. The title very often had a warlike image, and some Jews believed that the Messiah would in a literal sense free Israel from oppression.

Luke does not use this title very often, only at important moments: for example, at Jesus' birth he is described by the angels as 'Christ the Lord' (Luke 2:11). The most important occasion when this title is used is at Caesarea Philippi, when Peter describes Jesus as the 'Christ of God' (Luke 9:20). At the crucifixion, the crowd states that if Jesus was the Christ he would be able to save himself (Luke 23:35).

Luke emphasises that Jesus was born in Bethlehem, the town known as the 'City of David'. The fact that Jesus was born there fulfils an Old Testament prophecy that the Messiah would be born in the City of David.

It was important to emphasise that Jesus was descended from King David because David was thought to be the most important king in the history of the nation. He had been chosen and anointed as King by the prophet Samuel, so linking Jesus to David strengthened his authority. Jesus is called 'Son of David' by the Blind Man in Luke 18:38.

### The Lord

The Greek word 'kyrios', 'Lord', is used throughout the Bible. Sometimes it means 'God'. By being described as the Lord, Jesus is linked directly to God. Among the gospel writers only Luke uses this title for Jesus. The angels use it in their announcement of the birth (Luke 2:11). Sometimes in Luke the title has the meaning of 'sir'.

### Objectives

Learn more of the titles used of Jesus.

Understand the significance for Jesus as Messiah.

### Research activity

Jesus was depicted by Luke as one who would bring salvation. What does the world need saving from today?

### Beliefs and teachings

He called out, 'Jesus, Son of David, have mercy on me!'

Those who led the way rebuked him and told him to be quiet, but he shouted all the more, 'Son of David, have mercy on me!'

*Luke* 18:38–39

### Beliefs and teachings

Today in the town of David a Savior has been born to you; he is Christ the Lord.

*Luke* 2:1

## Son of Man

The title 'Son of Man' comes from the Book of Daniel in the Old Testament. It is also found in other Jewish literature. The phrase has two meanings. One is 'son of a man': that is, a human being, a person. The other meaning describes a mysterious figure, the Son of Man, who was believed to be close to God and who would come when the world was going to be judged. The title was also used in literature to describe one who would suffer.

Jesus refers to himself as the Son of Man, and it seems that he preferred to use this title. It is highly likely that Jesus used it because of the double meaning of the phrase, to prevent those who were his enemies from being able to accuse him of blasphemy. He also used it to emphasise his authority: for example, when he was criticised for his disciples picking corn on the Sabbath he replied, 'The Son of Man is Lord of the Sabbath' (Luke 6:5).

<aside>
**AQA   Examiner's tip**

You will be expected to be able to explain these titles and show how Jesus' life and ministry allowed all thee titles to be applied to him.
</aside>

**A**   The 'Son of Man'

### Activities

1   Read the passage in Isaiah 53 about the Suffering Servant. Make a table showing in one column what happens to the Servant. As you study the Gospel of Luke, add to the table incidents from Jesus' life that are similar.

2   How does Luke make it clear that he believed Jesus was the Son of God?

3   Why would it have been dangerous for Jesus to describe himself as the Son of God?

4   Jesus described himself as Son of Man. What did this mean?

5   What do Christians feel the world should be saved from today?

### Summary

You should now understand that Luke records a number of titles for Jesus that show Jesus' authority and his close relationship with God.

# John the Baptist

## The role of the prophet

John's father, Zechariah, was a priest in the Temple, but it was John's vocation to take the role of prophet. Zechariah had been told by an angel that John would be filled with the Holy Spirit:

> 66 *Many of the people of Israel will he bring back to the Lord their God. And he will go on before the Lord, in the spirit and power of Elijah, to turn the hearts of the fathers to their children and the disobedient to the wisdom of the righteous – to make ready a people prepared for the Lord.* 99
>
> *Luke* 1:16

Christians believe John played an important role in the coming of the Messiah. It was like that of Elijah: in Jewish tradition, it is believed that Elijah will appear before the Messiah. That is why at every Passover a spare chair is set and a glass of wine poured for Elijah.

John's message to the people was blunt. He left them in no doubt what was expected, and he knew that it was his role to point to the coming of the Messiah.

John stands in a line of Jewish prophets who spoke of justice and the importance of living according to God's law, and who suffered as a result.

## Baptism in the River Jordan

As an adult, John began to teach in the desert around the River Jordan. The people went to him in large numbers, even though his message was not comfortable. Many who came to hear John preach were baptised by him in the River Jordan.

Baptism was common in Israel in the 1st century CE. John used the River Jordan and only adults would have been baptised. During baptism the candidate would have entered the river and been completely covered with water. Baptism was part of the preparation people made for the coming of the Messiah. Baptism was also a sign of repentance.

## John's message

The crowd wondered whether John was the expected Messiah. John assured them that he was not. He said:

> 66 I baptise you with water. But one more powerful than I will come, the thongs of whose sandals I am not worthy to untie. He will baptise you with the Holy Spirit and with fire. His winnowing fork is in his hand to clear his threshing-floor and to gather the wheat into his barn, but he will burn up the chaff with unquenchable fire. 99
>
> *Luke* 3:16–17

### Objectives

Know about John the Baptist.

Understand how he prepared the way for Jesus as Messiah.

### Key terms

**Baptism**: a) the sacrament through which people become members of the church; b) in Luke's Gospel, John the Baptist used baptism as a way of washing away sins in readiness for the coming of the Messiah. He also baptised Jesus, though this was not connected with the washing away of sin.

**Repentence**: saying sorry and acknowledging to God that a believer has done wrong.

**A** *The River Jordan*

John called the people a 'brood of vipers' – not the best way to endear yourself to your hearers! He told them that just being Jewish and the children of Abraham would not save them from the judgement that was coming. John was clearly telling the people how powerful the Messiah would be.

When the people asked what they should do, John told them:

- The people were to share with one another – their clothing and food.
- Tax collectors were not to take more than was due to them. (Tax collectors were Jews who worked for Roman agents and most would collect more taxes than were owed in order to make a profit for themselves and their leaders.)
- Soldiers should not extort money or intimidate and should be satisfied with their pay.

### Repentance and forgiveness

John clearly had a strong sense of justice and fairness. He urged repentance, so that sins could be forgiven. He even challenged the royal family, condemning the king, Herod Antipas, for having an affair with his sister-in-law. This challenge was to lead to John's death.

## ■ Imprisonment and execution

Because of his willingness to criticise Herod publicly, John was arrested and imprisoned. While he was in prison, John sent a message to Jesus, asking Jesus whether he was the Messiah.

Jesus answered: 'The blind receive sight, the lame walk, those who have leprosy are cured, the deaf hear, the dead are raised and the good news is preached to the poor.' (Luke 7:22)

John was beheaded at the request of Herod's wife, after Herod had been entranced by the dance of Salome, her daughter. We know this from Mark's and Matthew's gospels (Mark 6:14–29, Matthew 14:1–2) and from Josephus, a Jewish historian of the 1st century.

**B**  *What John the Baptist might have looked like?*

# 3.3 The baptism of Jesus

## Jesus is baptised

> *When all the people were being baptised, Jesus was baptised too. And as he was praying, heaven was opened and the Holy Spirit descended on him in bodily form like a dove. And a voice came from heaven: 'You are my Son, whom I love; with you I am well pleased.'*
>
> *Luke 3:21–22*

**Objectives**

Learn about the baptism of Jesus and its significance for Christians.

Understand the importance of the baptism in showing that Jesus' authority came from God.

This is a very short account of the baptism of Jesus, but the description shows Jesus being given the full authority of God. In these few words Luke makes it clear to his readers that Jesus is the Messiah.

- Jesus is said to have been at prayer during the baptism.
- The heavens opening would be understood as a sign of God's presence.
- The Holy Spirit descends on Jesus like a dove. The dove is a very common image of God in religious traditions of the near east. For **Christians** the dove is a symbol of peace and of the Holy Spirit.
- The voice from heaven would be widely recognised as a sign from God of Jesus' authority.
- Jesus is described as 'my Son'. This is a quotation from Psalm 2:7

> *I will proclaim the decree of the Lord: He said to me, 'You are my Son; today I have become your father.'*
>
> *Psalms 2:7*

**Key terms**

**Christian**: someone who believes in Jesus Christ and follows the religion based on his teaching.

## ∞ links

In the account of the transfiguration in Luke 9 (see pages 72–73), there is another example of a voice from heaven and Jesus being described as 'my Son'.

## The meaning of baptism

Baptism is a sign of belonging. Christians in many traditions are baptised. In some churches baptism can be performed at any age, and babies may be baptised.

**A** *1st-century baptistery in Israel. John baptised in the river but others were baptised in such places as this*

In the ceremony of baptism there is a continuous link right back to the beginning of Christianity when Jesus was baptised. It is not known whether or not the disciples of Jesus were baptised by John the Baptist.

## Believer's baptism

Some people are baptised as adults, and this is known as 'believer's baptism'. Believer's baptism requires the person to declare publicly that they believe in God, and Jesus as the Son of God, with the Holy Spirit as God's presence in the world. They also declare that they repent of their sins. They are then completely submerged in water. This may be a river, but in Baptist and some other churches there is a baptistery (pool) for the purpose.

**B**   *Adult baptism*

The submerging is a sign of death and the coming up out of the water is a sign of rising to new life. In being baptised as a believer, the person is sharing in the death and Resurrection of Jesus.

## Infant baptism

When babies are baptised, godparents make promises on their behalf. The parents and the godparents affirm that they believe in the Father, the Son and the Holy Spirit, and then promise to bring the baby up to believe in the Christian faith and take their place in the worshipping community of the church.

When children are older and decide that they want to make these promises for themselves, they are offered another service, Confirmation.

There are religious symbols and symbolic actions in infant baptism.

- Promises are made by the parents and godparents to bring the child up in the Christian faith.
- The sign of the cross is made on the baby's head, sometimes with oil that has been blessed (anointing).
- A small amount of water is then dropped onto the baby's head three times, usually with the words: 'I baptise you in the name of the Father, the Son and the Holy Spirit.' The water represents cleansing from sin.
- Prayers are said, and the baby is welcomed into the family of the church.

**C**   *A baby being baptised*

**AQA**   *Examiner's tip*

If you answer a question on baptism today remember the two types: adult (believer's) and infant.

### Activities

1. John baptised only adults. Should babies be baptised?
2. How does the baptism indicate the beginning of Jesus' ministry?
3. What authority does the baptism narrative give Jesus?
4. Why do you think a dove was used to symbolise God's spirit?
5. 'The voice from heaven gave Jesus all the authority he needed.' Do you agree? Give reasons for your answer.

*Summary*

You should now know of Jesus' baptism and the authority it gave him and understand how modern baptism has developed.

# 3.4 The temptations

## Jesus in the desert

> ❝ *Jesus, full of the Holy Spirit, returned from the Jordan and was led by the Spirit in the desert, where for forty days he was tempted by the devil. He ate nothing during those days, and at the end of them he was hungry. The devil said to him, 'If you are the Son of God, tell this stone to become bread.' Jesus answered, 'It is written: "Man does not live on bread alone."' The devil led him up to a high place and showed him in an instant all the kingdoms of the world. And he said to him, 'I will give you all their authority and splendour, for it has been given to me, and I can give it to anyone I want to. So if you worship me, it will all be yours.' Jesus answered, 'It is written: "Worship the Lord your God and serve him only."' The devil led him to Jerusalem and had him stand on the highest point of the temple. 'If you are the Son of God,' he said, 'throw yourself down from here. For it is written: "He will command his angels concerning you to guard you carefully; they will lift you up in their hands, so that you will not strike your foot against a stone."' Jesus answered, 'It says: "Do not put the Lord your God to the test."' When the devil had finished all this tempting, he left him until an opportune time.* ❞

*Luke* 4:1–13

Matthew, Mark and Luke place the temptations in their gospels after the baptism. There are three temptations and they are interpreted as showing possible ways in which Jesus could carry out his ministry.

Jesus was filled with the Holy Spirit after the baptism, and it is possible that he chose the desert as a place where he could think about his coming ministry. He needed to be in control of his ministry and not to fall into the temptations that might face him. Jesus' resolve was being tested, and so was his commitment to God's message.

### The desert

The desert was very important to the Jews. It reminded them of the time they spent in the wilderness after escaping from Egypt. They had many difficulties in the wilderness but believed that they were saved by God.

It was quite normal for religious teachers to spend time in the desert. John the Baptist worked in the desert, and in the early Christian Church monks would go to the desert in search of spiritual truth.

While in the desert, Jesus did not eat anything for forty days as part of his preparation for ministry. The number forty parallels the forty years the Israelites spent in the wilderness.

### Objectives

Know in detail the account of the temptations of Jesus.

Interpret the meanings of the temptations.

Consider the importance of the temptations for Christians today.

### Key terms

**The devil**: the evil force that tempts people, also known as Satan.

### AQA Examiner's tip

It is important that you learn *Luke's* version of the temptations.

### Research activity

Read the story of Moses leading the Jews through the desert in Exodus. Notice the way that the people had to rely on God for their needs.

**A** *The desert in Israel*

## The devil

The **devil** is depicted in many ways in the Bible. He is an 'accuser' in the Old Testament, and is allowed by God to make Job, a faithful Jew, very ill as a test of Job's faith. Job was urged by his friends and wife to curse God and die, thus taking the easy way out.

The devil played a similar role in the temptations – he was pressing Jesus to take the easy route to popularity and testing his faith in God.

## The three temptations

### 'Turn these stones into bread'

In Jesus' time shortage of food was very often a problem. Jesus could easily have gained followers by feeding people. The devil told him to turn the stones into bread. Jesus' answer was very clear and based on the Old Testament: 'Man does not live on bread alone' (Deut 8:3). Jesus meant that there is more to life than satisfying physical needs.

### 'If you worship me, it will all be yours'

This temptation was encouraging Jesus to follow a political route to power. The devil believed that he could give Jesus authority. Jesus again used an Old Testament quotation to support his argument (Deuteronomy 6:13).

### 'So that you will not strike your foot against a stone'

Here the devil quoted the Old Testament at Jesus as part of the temptation (Psalm 91:11–12). Jesus' answer was very clear: he would not undertake something dramatic and showy to gain fame and influence.

The devil then left Jesus, but Luke says that it was only 'until an opportune time', indicating that this would not be the last time Jesus was tempted. By resisting temptations that would have set him on the wrong track as he began his ministry, Jesus set an example and acted as a role model for those around him and for all Christians.

## ◼ Temptations today

Christians are taught to be aware of temptations. One example is the desire for more and more material possessions. Christianity does not teach in a simple way that possessions are wrong; it is obsession with them that can lead to problems.

**B**  *Temptation can take the form of materialism*

Christians are faced with other temptations from time to time. They can involve any form of moral wrongdoing, lying, adultery, theft… the list is endless.

Jesus would not use a wrong method to further his message. He had been called in his baptism to bring people closer to God, but he would not use bribery or magic or worshipping the devil to achieve this.

### Summary

You should now know the temptations of Jesus and their meaning and be able to explain the importance of this account for Christians today.

### Activities

**1**  Jesus is said to have survived in the desert for 40 days without food. If this were not historically accurate, why might Luke have chosen to mention it?

**2**  How is the devil depicted in religion and religious art? Give reasons why you think he is seen in these ways.

**3**  Does belonging to a community like the Church help people deal with temptation? Explain the reasons for your answer.

**4**  Interview a Christian. How do they understand the Holy Spirit? What is their view of temptation?

### Discussion activity

Discuss in the class what temptations exist in society today. Should Christians set an example?

### Faith and healing

This is not the first healing story in Luke, but it is important because it demonstrates the link between **faith** and healing. It shows the authority with which Jesus worked and the different reactions he got from those around him. It is the first time that the Pharisees are mentioned in Luke's Gospel.

### The paralysed man

> ❝ One day as he was teaching, Pharisees and teachers of the law, who had come from every village of Galilee and from Judea and Jerusalem, were sitting there. And the power of the Lord was present for him to heal the sick. Some men came carrying a paralytic on a mat and tried to take him into the house to lay him before Jesus. When they could not find a way to do this because of the crowd, they went up on the roof and lowered him on his mat through the tiles into the middle of the crowd, right in front of Jesus.
>
> When Jesus saw their faith, he said, 'Friend, your sins are forgiven.'
>
> The Pharisees and the teachers of the law began thinking to themselves, 'Who is this fellow who speaks blasphemy? Who can forgive sins but God alone?'
>
> Jesus knew what they were thinking and asked, 'Why are you thinking these things in your hearts? Which is easier: to say, "Your sins are forgiven," or to say, "Get up and walk"? But that you may know that the Son of Man has authority on earth to forgive sins….' He said to the paralysed man, 'I tell you, get up, take your mat and go home.' Immediately he stood up in front of them, took what he had been lying on and went home praising God. Everyone was amazed and gave praise to God. They were filled with awe and said, 'We have seen remarkable things today.' ❞
>
> *Luke* 5:17–26

Mark says that this parable took place in Capernaum. A typical house in that part of Galilee in the 1st century would have had a flat roof.

As usual, Jesus was surrounded by crowds while he was teaching. This time the crowd include Pharisees and teachers of the Law.

Jesus was faced with what appeared to be a straightforward request for healing. The men in the story were convinced that Jesus could cure their friend. Jesus' response was immediate: he told the man that his sins were forgiven.

#### Sin and suffering

Most Jews at that time held the view that sin led to suffering. Therefore if Jesus forgave his sins, the man would get better. However, Jesus' authority to forgive sins was questioned.

### Objectives

Know the narrative of the paralysed man and understand how it demonstrated the authority of Jesus.

Recognise the reaction of Jesus' opponents and others.

### Key terms

**Faith:** belief and trust in someone, for example, Jesus.

### ⬭⬭ links

Look back at pages 40–41 in Chapter 2 to see more on the titles of Jesus given in the birth narratives.

Luke reports that the scribes and Pharisees began to question Jesus' authority. They were of the view that only God could forgive sin and therefore, by claiming to be able to forgive sin, Jesus was guilty of blasphemy.

Jesus asked them the question whether it was easier to forgive sins or to heal. To demonstrate his authority he turned and healed the man.

The crowd then went away giving praise to God and saying that they had seen remarkable things that day. They had seen a miracle. Jesus had demonstrated authority and challenged the Pharisees.

## ◼ The authority of the Son of Man

Jesus told the scribes and Pharisees, 'The Son of Man has authority on earth to forgive sins.' He then told the paralysed man to take up his mat and go home. Jesus had used a messianic title in describing himself as the 'Son of Man', having authority on earth.

In Daniel 7 there is a reference to a son of man. Daniel has a dream, or vision, of four beasts: a lion with the wings of an eagle, a bear, a leopard with four wings and four heads, and a beast with iron teeth and ten horns.

Daniel then describes a vision of God and reports, 'I looked and there before me was one like a son of man, coming from with the clouds of Heaven … He was given authority, glory and sovereign power' (Daniel 7:13–14). Jesus and many of his hearers would have known this meaning of the phrase Son of Man.

Some scholars are sure that Jesus was claiming that he was the Messiah here. He could have been accused of blasphemy for this, but the text records that this did not happen.

**A** *The healing of the paralysed man*

### Activities

1. Imagine you were there. What would you think as the dust from the roof began to fall on Jesus and the crowd?
2. What do you think the house owner would have thought?
3. How did the friends of the paralysed man demonstrate their faith?
4. Do you think the man on the stretcher had faith? Explain your answer.
5. How did Jesus demonstrate his authority?

### Summary

You should now know the story of the paralysed man, how Jesus demonstrated his authority and the reaction of the people there.

# Jesus' teaching on forgiveness

## Belief in God's forgiveness

**Forgiveness** was a well-established belief in Judaism in Jesus' time. The Jews wanted to be forgiven by God for their sins. Indeed, the whole of Jewish history throughout the Old Testament was seen as God forgiving the people over and over again.

### The Day of Atonement

A major Jewish festival each year was the Day of Atonement. On this day the High Priest would take a goat and lay his hands on its head. The goat would then be driven into the wilderness, and with it would go all the sins of the nation. This was the most solemn part of the festival, and people felt cleansed and forgiven afterwards.

## Jesus' message

Jesus told Peter that he should forgive not seven times but seventy times seven (Matthew 18:22). Jesus' message was that forgiveness from God is unlimited.

Jesus taught that God's forgiveness was for everyone, including outsiders and Gentiles. Those who were not born Jews, such as the centurion (Luke 7:1–10), also experienced his power.

Jesus set the example of forgiving sinners and welcoming them (Luke 6:29). It was important to him that they experienced the effects of God's forgiveness (such as the Sinful Woman in Luke 7:47). God's forgiveness was not limited to those with the correct lifestyle.

Jesus demonstrated that forgiveness from God could take the form of a sense of wellbeing, or more dramatically, the curing of illness.

In Luke 6:37, Jesus taught that people should not judge others. 'Do not judge and you will not be judged. Do not condemn, and you will not be condemned. Forgive, and you will be forgiven.' Jesus is clearly teaching here that forgiveness should be part of a believer's way of life.

In Luke 23:34 Jesus sets another example of forgiveness. As he was crucified he is quoted as saying, 'Father forgive them, for they do not know what they are doing.'

### Forgiveness and repentance

Central to the belief in forgiveness is the idea of repentance. People need to acknowledge that they have committed sins and must seek God's forgiveness. God will then forgive them.

Jesus' teaching in Luke 17:3–4 is very clear,

> 66 *If your brother sins, rebuke him, and if he repents, forgive him.* 99

Christians believe this is a powerful message for people.

**Objectives**

Learn about forgiveness as part of Jesus' teaching.

Understand how Jesus' ability to grant forgiveness was a sign of his being the Messiah and the Son of God.

**Key terms**

**Forgiveness:** to pardon a person for something that they have done wrong. In Biblical times, it was believed that only God could forgive sins.

**AQA  Examiner's tip**

You could be asked a question about Jesus and forgiveness. This is an example of a topic which can be found in more than one part of the specification.

## links

Jesus also taught about forgiveness in the parable of the Lost Son, see page 112.

At the very end of the gospel, Jesus gave his disciples their final instructions before leaving them. He told them,

> 66 *Repentance and forgiveness of sins shall be preached in his name to all nations.* 99
>
> *Luke* 24:47

**A**   *Many Christians go to the priest to confess their sins and seek forgiveness*

## Activities

1. Forgiveness is sometimes difficult. Who benefits from forgiveness – the forgiver or the forgiven?
2. Are there some things that cannot be forgiven?
3. If someone in prison asks for forgiveness and becomes a Christian, should the state forgive them?
4. How does the Christian teaching on forgiveness fit with the death penalty? Could a Christian ever support the death penalty?
5. Is forgiving the same as forgetting?

## Summary

You should now know and understand Jesus' teaching on forgiveness.

## ∞links

Jesus includes teaching about forgiveness in the Lord's Prayer (Luke 11:2–4). See Chapter 6.

### Extension activity

Interview a Christian church leader and ask about their understanding of forgiveness. How do they see their role in pronouncing forgiveness of sins, linking back to Jesus?

## Who am I?

> Once when Jesus was praying in private and his disciples were with him, he asked them, 'Who do the crowds say I am?' They replied, 'Some say John the Baptist; others say Elijah; and still others, that one of the prophets of long ago has come back to life.' 'But what about you?' he asked. 'Who do you say I am?'
>
> Peter answered, 'The Christ of God.' Jesus strictly warned them not to tell this to anyone. And he said, 'The Son of Man must suffer many things and be rejected by the elders, chief priests and teachers of the law, and he must be killed and on the third day be raised to life.' Then he said to them all: 'If anyone would come after me, he must deny himself and take up his cross daily and follow me.'
>
> *Luke* 9:18–23

### Objectives

Know and understand the conversation that led to Peter's declaring Jesus as the Christ.

Understand the importance of Peter's words.

This account of this incident is very important in understanding the person of Jesus and his authority. Some scholars have described this incident as the turning point of the Gospel. For the first time, the disciples began to recognise who Jesus was. They had been with him for some time, and had seen miracles and heard his teaching. Jesus now wanted to know whether they had understood what they had seen.

Luke records a number of occasions when Jesus prayed or taught about prayer, and here he is described as praying in private. Luke does not say where this incident took place, but Matthew and Mark state that it took place at Caesarea Philippi.

### Jesus' first question and the disciples' reply

When the disciples rejoined Jesus, he asked them what at first sight seems a simple question: 'Who do the crowds say that I am?' It was not an unnatural question, especially as he had just completed the miracle of the feeding of five thousand people with five loaves and two fishes.

The disciples offered Jesus three different answers.

- **John the Baptist.** This may seem an odd reply, given that John was still alive but in prison. Nevertheless, it is quite likely that the crowds were saying this. They might not have known what had happened to John.

- **Elijah.** The crowd had thought that John the Baptist was Elijah, preparing the way for the Messiah. They could easily have thought this about Jesus too.

- **One of the prophets of long ago comes back to life.** Again, it is not difficult to see why the crowds said this. If it was possible for Elijah to return to announce the coming of the Messiah, it was equally possible that Jesus might be another prophet from the past. That Jesus was acting like a prophet in pointing out the importance of living correctly and doing the will of God would have led to this answer.

**A** *Caesarea Philippi – the traditional site of Peter's confession*

### Jesus' second question and Peter's declaration

Jesus then asked the disciples: 'What about you? Who do you say I am?' Peter declared, 'The Christ of God.'

Peter recognised that there was something very different about Jesus. He at once described him as 'christos', the Anointed One – the Greek translation of the Hebrew word 'Messiah'. Peter's declaration is all the more important because a 1st-century Jewish speaker would normally avoid using the word 'God'.

Peter had recognised that Jesus' actions had the authority of God. In using the word 'Christ' he showed that he knew Jesus was a special person, with authority far beyond normal human authority. To have been anointed meant to have been chosen by God.

## ■ The Messiah

This episode in Jesus' ministry is very important when studying the disciples' understanding of who Jesus was, and what sort of a Messiah he might be. Peter recognised Jesus as a spiritual Messiah. He may have wondered whether Jesus was also going to be a political Messiah.

Jesus instructed the disciples to tell no one about this incident. It is possible that he knew how dangerous it might be to be openly recognised as the Messiah, especially if he was thought to be a political or warlike Messiah.

The idea that Jesus was a political Messiah may explain why Judas handed him over to the authorities later in his life, when he realised that Jesus was not going to lead a rebellion against the Romans. Judas may have been one of the revolutionaries in Israel who wanted the Romans to be overthrown.

**B** *Artist's impression of St Peter*

> **AQA** *Examiner's tip*
>
> Remember that Christ is not Jesus' surname. It really should be written 'Jesus the Christ' – Jesus the Anointed.

### Activities

1. Why do you think Jesus asked: 'Who do the crowds say that I am?'
2. What is the importance of Peter using the word 'Christ'?
3. How do you think Jesus felt when he heard the words of Peter?
4. Suggest reasons why Jesus strictly warned the disciples not to tell anyone that he was the Christ of God.
5. Does authority come from a title? Is there more to it than that?

### Discussion activity

What do you think a Christian can do today to 'take up his cross daily and follow me'?

### Summary

You should now know that Peter declared Jesus to be the Anointed One, the Christ of God, and that this means he recognised Jesus' authority.

# 3.8 The transfiguration

## The voice from the cloud

> 66 *About eight days after Jesus said this, he took Peter, John and James with him and went up onto a mountain to pray. As he was praying, the appearance of his face changed, and his clothes became as bright as a flash of lightning. Two men, Moses and Elijah, appeared in glorious splendour, talking with Jesus. They spoke about his departure, which he was about to bring to fulfilment at Jerusalem. Peter and his companions were very sleepy, but when they became fully awake, they saw his glory and the two men standing with him. As the men were leaving Jesus, Peter said to him, 'Master, it is good for us to be here. Let us put up three shelters – one for you, one for Moses and one for Elijah.' (He did not know what he was saying.) While he was speaking, a cloud appeared and enveloped them, and they were afraid as they entered the cloud. A voice came from the cloud, saying, 'This is my Son, whom I have chosen; listen to him.' When the voice had spoken, they found that Jesus was alone. The disciples kept this to themselves, and told no one at that time what they had seen.* 99
>
> *Luke* 9:28–36

### Objectives

Know the story of the transfiguration.

Understand the importance of the transfiguration.

### Key terms

**Transfiguration**: an incident in the New Testament when Jesus was lit up by divine light, through which the divinity of Jesus was revealed.

Just as at the baptism, there was a voice from heaven. This time it came from a cloud that covered all of them. The voice described Jesus as 'my Son, whom I have chosen'. The disciples were told to listen to him. It was clear that, as God's Son, Jesus had very special authority from God.

Peter's words are an indication of his character as shown in the Gospel. He sometimes spoke without thinking and was impetuous. Peter, John and James were the only disciples to witness this event (just as in the healing of Jairus' daughter).

After all this the disciples were silent – probably shocked – and left without words. We are informed that they did not tell anyone about the incident.

### Research activity

Find out what Jewish families do at Sukkoth.

### A flash of lightning

The **transfiguration** is an incident when Jesus' appearance changed. Luke informs us that Jesus' face and clothes became 'as bright as a flash of lightning'.

In Christian literature, white was a sign of heavenly presence. Angels wore white garments and citizens of heaven were believed to wear white.

### The Tabernacle

This incident is a reference to the Exodus, when the cloud of God's presence was described as hovering over the Tabernacle in the camp in the wilderness. The Tabernacle was the tent within which the tablets of the Law were kept and was a holy place.

**A** *Jewish family at Sukkoth*

## Moses and Elijah

Moses and Elijah were two of the most important Jews mentioned in the Old Testament.

- Moses led the Exodus of the Hebrews from Egypt to the Promised Land and received the Ten Commandments from God.
- Elijah was one of the great prophets who, as we have already seen (pages 70–71), was important to Jewish Messianic hopes.

Moses represents the Law and Elijah represents the prophets. Their presence here was a sign that Jesus was completing the work of the Law and the prophets in bringing the people back to God.

### The importance of the transfiguration

This passage is an important event in the disciples' developing understanding of the authority of Jesus.

- The voice from heaven again emphasises Jesus' authority and the fact that he is God's son. In the transfiguration the disciples are spoken to directly, whereas at the baptism only Jesus heard the voice.
- The event for the disciples is a foreshadowing of Jesus' glory after the Resurrection, and a vision of heaven.
- Religious symbols – light, the voice from heaven and the cloud – emphasise the presence of God.
- Major Old Testament figures emphasise that Jesus stands in the tradition of the Law and the prophets.

**B**  *Artistic depiction of the transfiguration*

Luke sometimes gives details of times and places, and sometimes he does not. The text tells us that this happened eight days after Jesus had the conversation with his disciples about who he was.

AQA  **Examiner's tip**

In addition to being asked to describe the event, you may be asked to explain its importance.

### Activities

1. What signs of the presence of God are there in the transfiguration narrative?
2. How does the transfiguration emphasise the authority of Jesus?
3. Why do you think all three synoptic gospel writers thought that it was important to include the transfiguration in the gospels?
4. How would the story help those who were feeling pressured in life?
5. Keep a list of the times in Luke's Gospel that Peter is the first of the disciples to speak out – sometimes without thinking.

### Summary

You should now know the narrative of the transfiguration, and understand how it is used by Luke to emphasise that Jesus is a man of prayer who has clear authority from God.

# 3.9 | Martha and Mary

## Jesus' visit

> ❝ As Jesus and his disciples were on their way, he came to a village where a woman named Martha opened her home to him. She had a sister called Mary, who sat at the Lord's feet listening to what he said. But Martha was distracted by all the preparations that had to be made. She came to him and asked, 'Lord, don't you care that my sister has left me to do the work by myself? Tell her to help me!' 'Martha, Martha,' the Lord answered, 'you are worried and upset about many things, but only one thing is needed. Mary has chosen what is better, and it will not be taken away from her.' ❞
>
> *Luke* 10:38–42

### Objectives

Study the incident of Martha and Mary.

Understand Luke's description of Jesus' treatment of women.

Understand the meaning of 'Lord' as title for Jesus.

Understand the significance of this story for Christians.

According to John's gospel, Martha and Mary lived in Bethany, about two miles from Jerusalem. Jesus and the disciples were travelling towards Jerusalem and perhaps Jesus knew what awaited him there. They stopped at Martha's house, which she shared with her sister Mary. While they are there, Mary behaved in a way that would have been considered inappropriate.

### Key terms

**Lord**: this was a messianic title given to Jesus by the early Church after his ressurection. By the time Luke wrote his Gospel, the title was in common use, so Luke uses it.

### A woman's place

In 1st-century Palestine, the place of women was in the domestic area and with the children. The men would sit in the public area and debate and argue. Mary is described as sitting with the men and listening to Jesus teaching. She is behaving like a man when she should be doing women's work.

Martha is well aware of this. It may be true that the preparation for the meal was a difficult task. Her major concern, however, may have been the awkward social position that Mary has taken.

Jesus is sympathetic but tells Martha not to fuss. Mary has chosen something better – she has chosen to listen to the teaching about the Kingdom of God – and this should not be taken away from her. This can be interpreted to mean that once she has heard the message it will stay with her, whatever happens.

Jesus is shown in Luke as being very concerned for the place of women. Luke sees women as important to the narrative and part of God's creation. Women feature prominently in the life of Jesus and are also used in the parables to illustrate his teaching. Christians can learn from this that women have a full part to play in the church and in society. Jesus was not making a statement about women's rights – he was emphasising God's teaching that all people matter equally.

A Location of Jerusalem and Bethany

## Martha and Mary

Some scholars have seen the difference between Mary and Martha as one that shows different styles of belief. Some people are very active (Martha) but others are more thoughtful and contemplative (Mary).

People need to be a bit of both: 'Without the first you wouldn't eat, without the second you would not worship' (T Wright, *Luke for Everyone*).

## Jesus as Lord

In the passage Jesus is described as '**Lord**' twice. In the Old Testament, the word for 'Lord' occurs over 9,000 times and almost always refers to God.

Luke uses the word more often than anyone else in the New Testament. It can be a way of addressing Jesus politely (or anyone else for that matter), but it can also mean that people recognised Jesus as someone God-like.

Later writers in the New Testament refer to Jesus as Lord, indicating that Jesus is the one who rose from the dead.

AQA    *Examiner's tip*

The titles of Jesus are important in understanding Christian beliefs about who Jesus was. Make sure that you learn the ones you have studied and their meaning.

**B**  *Jesus in the house of Martha and Mary*

**Research activity**

1  Look up some other references to women in the Gospel of Luke and explain to a partner what you have learned.

2  Make notes on the passages that you have studied.

Luke 7:11; Luke 7:32; Luke 8:2; Luke 13:11; Luke 15:8ff; Luke 18:1ff; Luke 21:1–4; Luke 23:27ff

**Summary**

You should now know an incident when Jesus was called Lord and the significance of this title and understand that Jesus respected women and valued those who made time to consider spiritual issues.

**Activities**

1  Why was Martha upset with Mary?
2  What does Jesus' reply teach about his attitude to women?

**3**

### The authority of Jesus – summary

For the examination you should now be able to:

✔ explain the role of John the Baptist in preparing the way for Jesus

✔ know and explain the baptism and temptations of Jesus

✔ understand the titles of Jesus – Lord, Christ/Messiah, Son of Man, Son of God – and their importance

✔ know and understand the stories of the healing of the paralysed man, Peter's declaration, the transfiguration, and Martha and Mary as they show different titles of Jesus

✔ explain the importance of the stories you have studied for a Christian understanding of Jesus and his teaching.

#### Sample answer

1 Write an answer to the following examination question:

How did Luke show that Jesus had authority among people? *(6 marks)*

2 Read the following sample answer:

'Luke showed that Jesus had authority from the beginning. In the announcement of his birth, Gabriel said that he would be the Son of God. Later at the baptism there was a voice from heaven which said, 'You are my son: I am pleased with you.' Jesus then got the idea that he was specially sent from God. Later Jesus was faced with a man who had been lowered through the roof and he said that his sins were forgiven. The Pharisees questioned this and Jesus said that to show he had authority to forgive sins he would tell the man to walk away. He did this and the crowd were amazed. Jews believed that sin led to suffering. Later there was another voice from heaven. At the transfiguration Jesus and the disciples were covered by a cloud (sign of God) and the voice this time told the disciples to listen to Jesus. In these ways Luke showed that Jesus had authority as the Messiah.'

3 With a partner, discuss the sample answer. Do you think that there are other things that the student could have included in the answer?

4 What mark would you give this out of 6? Look at the mark scheme in the Introduction on page 7 (AO1). What are the reasons for the mark you have given?

# AQA Examination-style questions

Look at this picture and
answer the following questions.

**1** Describe in detail the baptism of Jesus. *(4 marks)*

**2** How did John the Baptist prepare the way for Jesus? *(4 marks)*

**3** Give two of the temptations of Jesus and explain what each means. *(4 marks)*

**4** **(a)** Describe briefly what happened when Jesus visited Martha and Mary's house. *(2 marks)*

    **(b)** Why was Mary's action criticised by Martha? *(2 marks)*

    **(c)** How did Jesus respond to Martha's criticism of Mary? *(2 marks)*

**5** What do the titles of Jesus tell people about who he was? *(6 marks)*

**6** Describe in detail the transfiguration of Jesus. *(6 marks)*

**7** 'The baptism is all that is needed to demonstrate that Jesus is the Messiah.'
Do you agree? Give reasons for your answer, showing that you have thought
about more than one point of view. *(6 marks)*

# 4 The suffering, death and resurrection of Jesus

## 4.1    The Last Supper

### ▌ The Feast of Passover

> 66 *Then came the day of Unleavened Bread on which the Passover lamb had to be sacrificed. Jesus sent Peter and John, saying, 'Go and make preparations for us to eat the Passover.'*
>
> *'Where do you want us to prepare for it?' they asked.*
>
> *He replied, 'As you enter the city, a man carrying a jar of water will meet you. Follow him to the house that he enters, and say to the owner of the house, "The Teacher asks: Where is the guest room, where I may eat the Passover with my disciples?" He will show you a large upper room, all furnished. Make preparations there.'*
>
> *They left and found things just as Jesus had told them. So they prepared the Passover.*
>
> *When the hour came, Jesus and his apostles reclined at the table. And he said to them, 'I have eagerly desired to eat this Passover with you before I suffer. For I tell you, I will not eat it again until it finds fulfilment in the kingdom of God.'*
>
> *After taking the cup, he gave thanks and said, 'Take this and divide it among you. For I tell you I will not drink again of the fruit of the vine until the kingdom of God comes.'*
>
> *And he took bread, gave thanks and broke it, and gave it to them, saying, 'This is my body given for you; do this in remembrance of me.'*
>
> *In the same way, after the supper he took the cup, saying, 'This cup is the new covenant in my blood, which is poured out for you. But the hand of him who is going to betray me is with mine on the table. The Son of Man will go as it has been decreed, but woe to that man who betrays him.' They began to question among themselves which of them it might be who would do this. 99*
>
> *Luke 22:7–23*

The Feast of Unleavened Bread refers to the Passover, which was about to be celebrated. This was to take place in an upper room. It is likely that Jesus knew who the owner of the room was because he described him as a man who would be carrying a jar of water. This would have been unusual, as collecting water was a woman's job.

Jesus said of the Passover, 'I will not eat it again until it finds fulfilment in the kingdom of God.' He knew that suffering faced him.

### Objectives

Learn about the Last Supper.

Understand the words and actions of Jesus.

Understand how the Last Supper is important for Christians today.

### ∞ links

See the Glossary on page 140 for definition of aspostles.

### AQA    Examiner's tip

It is essential that you know this passage and can retell it accurately for the examination.

## Jesus' words and actions

Jesus predicted his death and resurrection at the supper, but the disciples (here called apostles) did not understand this at the time.

There is a promise here for Christians about the future certainty of life after death. Jesus will die to create, once and for all, a link between God and believers. Believers will be able to rely on the promise that they have been saved, and God will welcome them into the kingdom of heaven.

**A**   *The Last Supper*

There is also a promise about the new covenant, or relationship with God. Jesus was contrasting the old covenant, which relied on people following the law, with the new covenant, the belief that God is a God who gives Christians forgiveness, and the power, through the Holy Spirit, to live out the Christian life.

### The Eucharist

During the Roman persecution, Christians often met in secret to repeat this meal. The Eucharist (literally 'thanksgiving') meal appears to have led to the early Christians being accused of cannibalism by their enemies, because they ate 'bodies' and drank 'blood'.

### The betrayal is foretold

Jesus does not mention Judas by name when he predicts that he will be betrayed. This prediction made the other disciples anxious, but Jesus is clear that he must face his certain death.

## The importance of the Last Supper

The Last Supper is remembered in churches that celebrate communion services. (Some Christian groups, like the Quakers [Society of Friends] and the Salvation Army, do not celebrate the communion, but almost all others do.)

In I Corinthians 11, Paul describes the Christian ceremony of the Eucharist and gives instructions on what should happen at the meal. It is clear from the writings of Paul that Jesus' actions became the pattern for Christians.

### The Last Supper remembered today

For many Christians today the celebration of the Eucharist gives them an opportunity to remember that Jesus died for their sins, and to give thanks to God for this and for the promise of new life that it brought. It also gives them a chance to re-enact the Last Supper and to feel that they are part of the modern community of disciples.

The elements are: wine, bread, giving thanks and sharing. The Minister or priest repeats the words of Jesus from the Last Supper. This reminds the congregation of the suffering of Jesus and the sacrifice that he made.

## links

Look back at pages 34–35 to revise the Exodus and the covenant.

### Research activity

Find out which Christian churches describe their service as: **Eucharist, Lord's Supper, Communion, Sacrament, Mass, Breaking of Bread**. Make a table to show which denominations use which description.

### Activities

1. How does Jesus link himself with the Passover sacrifice?
2. Why is it important that he encourages the disciples to share the meal?
3. Explain the meaning of the bread and the wine.
4. Explain the difference between the old covenant and the new covenant.
5. How does celebrating the communion service give Christians a sense of community?

### Summary

You will now know the story of the Last Supper and the importance of Jesus' words and actions. You will understand the importance of the story of the Last Supper for Christians today.

> 66 *Jesus went out as usual to the Mount of Olives, and his disciples followed him. On reaching the place, he said to them, 'Pray that you will not fall into temptation.' He withdrew about a stone's throw beyond them, knelt down and prayed, 'Father, if you are willing, take this cup from me; yet not my will, but yours be done.' An angel from heaven appeared to him and strengthened him. And being in anguish, he prayed more earnestly, and his sweat was like drops of blood falling to the ground.*
>
> *When he rose from prayer and went back to the disciples, he found them asleep, exhausted from sorrow. 'Why are you sleeping?' he asked them. 'Get up and pray so that you will not fall into temptation.'* 99
>
> *Luke* 22:39–46

## Objectives

Study the events that took place on the Mount of Olives.

Understand how these events formed part of the salvation work of Jesus.

Understand what these incidents might mean to Christians.

### Key terms

**Mount of Olives**: the hilly area outside Jerusalem that consisted of olive orchards. This was where Jesus spent time in prayer after the Last Supper and where he was arrested.

**Temptation**: a test of faith; being attracted to act in a wrong way, or being tested though suffering.

### ■ The Garden of Gethsemane

Luke states that Jesus and the disciples went to the **Mount of Olives**, which was to the east of Jerusalem. On the Mount of Olives was the Garden of Gethsemane. Although Luke does not record the name of the Garden of Gethsemane, it is clear from the other gospels that this is where Jesus and the disciples went after their Passover meal. It was to be the place of Jesus' arrest.

This passage is important in Luke's description of the Passion of Jesus and helps Christians to understand something of the turmoil that Jesus went though. Central to the passage is prayer – a strong Lukan theme. Jesus is said to have prayed fervently in the garden and to have encouraged his disciples to pray.

### ■ Jesus' prayer

Jesus is shown to be concerned for his disciples. When he tells them to pray that they will not 'fall into temptation', he may have been referring back to his temptations in the desert. Perhaps he was wanting his disciples to pray that they should not face those kinds of temptations.

The word '**temptation**' is also used in the Lord's Prayer, and many Christians believe that this was a prayer to God that they would not be persecuted. Luke would have known that the early Christians were being persecuted, so it would have been important to him to include Jesus' words that the disciples should not put to the test.

Jesus is said to have knelt in prayer, and this is why many Christian worshippers kneel to pray. Jews normally stand to pray.

**A** *The Garden of Gethsemane*

### ∞ links

For the Lord's Prayer in Luke, see pages 132–133.

**B**   *Jesus praying on the Mount of Olives*

## God's will

Jesus prayed that the 'cup' would be taken away from him. However, he was prepared to serve and to go through with the crucifixion because it was God's will – 'Not my will but yours be done.' There is an echo here of Jesus' mother's acceptance of her role in Jesus' birth: at the annunciation, Mary said, 'May it be to me as you have said.'

An angel appeared to Jesus. Even though he was clearly frightened, he was prepared to face whatever would come.

Jesus' prayer would have supported and inspired the early Christians as they faced persecution. If Jesus was prepared to do God's will, so also would Christians.

## The sleeping disciples

After he had finished praying, Jesus went back to the sleeping disciples. It is not surprising that they were sleepy, if they had drunk four glasses of wine and it was now late. Jesus again told them to pray that they would not be tested.

**Summary**

You should now know the incidents on the Mount of Olives leading to Jesus' arrest and understand the importance for Christians of Jesus' prayer.

## The betrayal

> " *While he was still speaking a crowd came up, and the man who was called Judas, one of the Twelve, was leading them. He approached Jesus to kiss him, but Jesus asked him, 'Judas, are you betraying the Son of Man with a kiss?'*
>
> *When Jesus' followers saw what was going to happen, they said, 'Lord, should we strike with our swords?' And one of them struck the servant of the high priest, cutting off his right ear.*
>
> *But Jesus answered, 'No more of this!' And he touched the man's ear and healed him.*
>
> *Then Jesus said to the chief priests, the officers of the temple guard, and the elders, who had come for him, 'Am I leading a rebellion, that you have come with swords and clubs? Every day I was with you in the temple courts, and you did not lay a hand on me. But this is your hour – when darkness reigns.'* "
>
> *Luke* 22:47–53

Judas has been blamed throughout history as the man who betrayed Jesus. The question is whether he had any choice. If Jesus was called by God to die in order to bring salvation, there had to be an arrest and a trial. If the word for 'betray' in Luke 22:48 is translated as 'handed over', then the sense of evil is lost.

### Judas

Judas almost certainly, along with some of the other disciples, thought that Jesus was a military or political Messiah. By bringing the authorities to him in the garden, Judas may well have expected or hoped that Jesus would declare the revolution to have begun.

Judas may have hoped that Jesus would lead his followers and get rid of the Romans. However, this was not to be.

### The Son of Man

Jesus described himself again as the Son of Man. At this most stressful and significant time, he uses the messianic title.

### The disciples

The disciples wanted to protect Jesus. Asking whether they should use their swords, and one of them cutting off the **High Priest**'s servant's ear, shows that some of them thought Jesus was going to fight the Romans. But Jesus was not a political Messiah, and Luke's use of the word 'darkness' shows that the disciples were wrong.

Darkness has a double meaning in this passage. It was actually physically dark at Jesus' arrest, but if the good news that Jesus was bringing about the Kingdom were to be lost this would create a spiritual darkness.

### Objectives

Know the incident of the arrest of Jesus.

Understand that it demonstrated that he was a peaceful Messiah.

### Key terms

**High Priest**: the High Priest was a special figure in the Jerusalem Temple. He often was also the leader of the Sanhedrin, the supreme council of the Jews. The High Priest who condemned Jesus to death was called Caiaphas.

### AQA Examiner's tip

Be prepared to answer a question on why Judas betrayed Jesus. You do not need to know the preparations Judas made.

**A**   *Judas betrays Jesus with a kiss*

In Luke 22:1–6 Judas' preparations to betray Jesus meant that he went to the chief priests and soldiers to discuss how Jesus should be handed over. They gave him money which he accepted and then began to look for his opportunity to betray Jesus away from the crowds.

*Luke 22:1–6*

## Betrayed by a kiss

In this incident, the kiss identifies Jesus and he is handed over to the authorities by one of his own followers.

It is not unusual in the Middle East to use a kiss in greeting, but it is ironic that Judas indicated who Jesus was by a kiss – a sign of affection.

**Discussion activity**

Discuss whether Judas had free will. Is he to blame for what happened to Jesus?

**Activities**

1   How did Judas identify Jesus?
2   Why do you think Jesus was arrested as a rebel?
3   What was Jesus' reaction to the disciples when they offered to fight?
4   'Jesus showed that he was a man of peace at his arrest.' How did he do this?

**Summary**

You should now know about the arrest of Jesus and the importance of the incident for an understanding of who Jesus was.

## ■ A delicate balance

The Jews had been successful in persuading the Roman authorities to let them worship God, and they had been allowed to keep the Temple and their own religious ruling council, the **Sanhedrin**. They were not required to worship the Emperor, and coins in Palestine did not carry the head of the Emperor. It was a delicate balance, and those in authority would not want this balance upset. There may have been personal animosity towards Jesus because in his preaching he had not always accepted the authority or judgement of those he met.

## ■ The trial before the Jewish Council

> 66 At daybreak the council of the elders of the people, both the chief priests and teachers of the law, met together, and Jesus was led before them. 'If you are the Christ,' they said, 'tell us.'
>
> Jesus answered, 'If I tell you, you will not believe me, and if I asked you, you would not answer. But from now on, the Son of Man will be seated at the right hand of the mighty God.'
>
> They all asked, 'Are you then the Son of God?'
>
> He replied, 'You are right in saying I am.'
>
> Then they said, 'Why do we need any more testimony? We have heard it from his own lips.' 99
>
> *Luke* 22:66–71

The Council was a body of people consisting of Chief Priests, Sadducees, Scribes and Pharisees – a combination of the powerful in the land of Israel. They asked Jesus if he was the Christ. Whatever Jesus had replied would have got him into trouble. If he said that he was, he would have been accused of blasphemy. If he said that he wasn't, they would have made trouble for him as an impostor. His reply reflected this difficulty.

Jesus told them that from that time on the Son of Man would be with God. The Council interpreted 'Son of Man' in a messianic sense, and then asked Jesus if he was the Son of God.

The translations are very important here. The Greek means 'You say that I am' but some versions of the Bible (for example, NIV) translate it as, 'You are right in saying that I am.' Whatever was actually said, the Council took Jesus' reply to mean that he was claiming to be the Son of God. This was blasphemy.

The Sanhedrin did not have the legal power to put Jesus to death. They needed the authority of Pilate.

**Objectives**

Know the trials of Jesus.

Understand why there are three different trials.

Understand the charges against Jesus.

Understand Jesus' approach to the trials and the links to his messianic claim.

**Key terms**

**Jewish Council (Sanhedrin):** the Supreme Council of the Jews consisted of 71 members, usually led by the High Priest, and who met in Jerusalem.

AQA **Examiner's tip**

You will need to be very clear about the trials – their order, the charges, and the actions of the Sanhedrin, Herod, Pilate and Jesus.

**A** *The ruins of the seat of the Sanhedrin*

## The first hearing before Pilate

> ❝ *Then the whole assembly rose and led him off to Pilate. And they began to accuse him, saying, 'We have found this man subverting our nation. He opposes payment of taxes to Caesar and claims to be Christ, a king.'*
>
> *So Pilate asked Jesus, 'Are you the king of the Jews?'*
> *'Yes, it is as you say,' Jesus replied.*
>
> *Then Pilate announced to the chief priests and the crowd, 'I find no basis for a charge against this man.'*
>
> *But they insisted, 'He stirs up the people all over Judea by his teaching. He started in Galilee and has come all the way here.'*
>
> *On hearing this, Pilate asked if the man was a Galilean. When he learned that Jesus was under Herod's jurisdiction, he sent him to Herod, who was also in Jerusalem at that time.* ❞
>
> *Luke* 23:1–7

Pontius Pilate was the Roman Governor and he was responsible for law and order. He also had the authority to sentence someone to death. The Council was determined that Jesus should die.

When Jesus was before Pilate, the charge was different. Pilate, as a Roman, would have had no interest in a charge of blasphemy, so the Sanhedrin spoke of Jesus encouraging revolts and opposing the tribute payment to Caesar (Luke 20:25).

They added that Jesus 'claims to be Christ, a king'. The name 'Christ', the anointed one, referred back to the kings of Israel being anointed, and they were accusing Jesus of wanting the power of a king.

These were political charges that they hoped Pilate could not afford to ignore.

Pilate asked Jesus, 'Are you the king of the Jews?' This was a dangerous question for Jesus because if he had said yes the charge would have been one of treason – of trying to overthrow the Romans. There were plenty of people from Galilee who wanted to do that.

Pilate found out that Jesus was a Galilean and, perhaps glad of an excuse not to hear this case, referred him to Herod the King – the ruler of Galilee. Pilate saw no reason for Jesus being charged.

## Jesus before Herod

Herod was allowed by the Romans to be a king, the ruler of Galilee. Jesus was abused by Herod, who mocked him by dressing him in a 'rich coat'.

Jesus did not speak. This reflects Isaiah 53, when it was predicted that the Suffering Servant would be silent. Jesus' accusers then sent him back to Pilate.

**Extension activity**

Look up what is known about the Sanhedrin and its powers. Why do you think they were so keen to have Jesus put to death?

**Activities**

1. What did the Jewish Council accuse Jesus of?
2. Why did the Council have to take Jesus to Pilate?
3. What charges did Jesus face before Pilate?
4. Why do you think Herod sent Jesus back to Pilate?

> ❝ *When Herod saw Jesus, he was greatly pleased, because for a long time he had been wanting to see him. From what he had heard about him, he hoped to see him perform some miracle. He plied him with many questions, but Jesus gave him no answer. The chief priests and the teachers of the law were standing there, vehemently accusing him. Then Herod and his soldiers ridiculed and mocked him. Dressing him in an elegant robe, they sent him back to Pilate. That day Herod and Pilate became friends – before this they had been enemies.* ❞
>
> *Luke* 23:8–12

**Summary**

You should now understand the reasons for the trials of Jesus before the Jewish Council, Pilate and Herod, and the charges brought. You will have considered Jesus' approach to his trials.

### The second trial before Pilate: Jesus is condemned

**Pontius Pilate** had a duty to uphold justice. Yet he had a problem: either he was true to himself and his duty and ignored the clamour for Jesus' death, or he gave in to the Jews. If he ignored the accusers, it was predictable that there would be trouble on the streets. He was used to that. If he gave in to the Jews, it meant that he would condemn an innocent man to die. Perhaps he sent Jesus to Herod in the hope that Herod would deal with the problem. Herod didn't.

**Case study**

### Pontius Pilate

Pontius Pilate was Governor of the Roman Province of Judea from 26 to 36 CE. The first century Jewish historians Philo and Josephus show him as inflexible, harsh, vindictive and cruel. He showed that he had little regard for Jewish traditions when he ordered his troops to enter Jerusalem carrying flagpoles bearing an image of the Emperor uncovered. The Jews protested and said that they would rather die than give up when threatened with death. It was Pilate that backed down and ordered the images to be removed from Jerusalem. On another occasion he had his troops beat those protesting about him, using money from the Temple to build a viaduct (Luke 13:1-2). Many of the protesters died.

Pilate was the Governor who released Barabbas at the trial of Jesus. Barabbas was in prison for murder and may have been a rebel against the Romans. Pilate had the power of life and death over people. There is no doubt that the early Christians regarded Pilate as a major player in the suffering of Jesus. Christians have believed from the beginning that Jesus suffered under Pontius Pilate. In Luke's version Pilate could find nothing for Jesus to answer at his trials and stated this three times (Luke 23:4. 23:14 and 23:16). In the second trial before Pilate, Jesus was ordered to be flogged but in the end Pilate gave in to the crowd and released Barabbas and handed Jesus to the Jewish authorities to do as they wished. Pilate's downfall came in 35 CE when he had a rebellion of Samaritans put down violently. The complaints from the Samaritans meant that he was sent back to Rome to answer for his actions. Later folklore says that Pontius Pilate died a miserable death.

Discuss with your teacher, 'Why do you think Luke went to great lengths to show that Pontius Pilate wanted to find Jesus not guilty?'

> 66 *Pilate called together the chief priests, the rulers and the people, and said to them, 'You brought me this man as one who was inciting the people to rebellion. I have examined him in your presence and have found no basis for your charges against him. Neither has Herod, for he sent him back to us; as you can see, he has done nothing to deserve death. Therefore, I will punish him and then release him.'*
>
> *With one voice they cried out, 'Away with this man! Release Barabbas to us!' (Barabbas had been thrown into prison for an insurrection in the city, and for murder.)*
>
> *Wanting to release Jesus, Pilate appealed to them again. But they kept shouting, 'Crucify him! Crucify him!'*
>
> *For the third time he spoke to them: 'Why? What crime has this man committed? I have found in him no grounds for the death penalty. Therefore I will have him punished and then release him.'*
>
> *But with loud shouts they insistently demanded that he be crucified, and their shouts prevailed. So Pilate decided to grant their demand. He released*

**A** Portrait of Pontius Pilate

> the man who had been thrown into prison for insurrection and murder, the one they asked for, and surrendered Jesus to their will. **"**
>
> *Luke* 23:13–25

Pilate could find no reason to sentence Jesus to death. His solution was to have Jesus flogged and released. He agreed with Herod that there were no grounds for capital punishment. Yet in the end Pilate gave in to the crowd's demands and handed Jesus over to the Jews to do what they wanted with him.

### The crowd

About a week earlier Jesus had entered Jerusalem and been greeted like a king. Now the crowd turned against him, and demanded the release of Barabbas, a rebel. Despite Pilate's offer to flog Jesus, they demanded that he be crucified.

### Barabbas

Luke reports that Barabbas had been arrested for 'an insurrection in the city, and for murder' – so unlike Jesus, Barabbas was a convicted criminal. There were many uprisings in Jerusalem, and Barabbas may well have been a member of one of the Zealot groups in the city.

There are no records in the ancient texts of prisoners being completely released at Passover time in Palestine. However, there is some evidence that Jewish prisoners were released for a few hours at Passover, and Luke may have been drawing from this tradition.

## ■ Jesus' conviction

The death penalty was usually only given to those who rebelled against Rome, and Jesus was executed as if he were a rebel. But look closely at Luke's text. Pilate never actually found Jesus guilty of anything. There is a debate to be had over who is to blame for Jesus' death.

- **Jesus** was sure that God was calling him to die for the sins of the world. It was all part of God's plan to save people. He therefore put himself in a position to be crucified, and did not defend himself or let the disciples defend him. He could have regarded himself as a martyr (a person who chooses to suffer for their beliefs).

- **Judas** handed Jesus over to the authorities. Had Judas not arranged the meeting on the Mount of Olives that night of the Passover, Jesus might not have been arrested.

- **Pilate** had a responsibility as a leader to uphold the Roman justice system. In the end, it appears that he just gave in to the crowds and the Jewish leaders. Had he acted in a just way, Jesus would have been released.

- **The members of the Jewish council** (the Sanhedrin) were determined to have Jesus convicted and sentenced to death because they believed he was guilty of blasphemy. Since they did not have that power, they changed the charge to one of treason and went to Pilate, who could pass the death sentence.

- **Herod** could have used what power he had to release Jesus. He was not interested in Jesus and sent him back to Pilate, with almost inevitable consequences.

- **The crowd** may or may not have understood what was going on, and could have been manipulated by the leaders. We will never know for sure.

**Discussion activity**

Discuss who you think was responsible for Jesus being crucified.

**Activities**

1. Did Pilate live up to his duty as Governor? Should people in public office always do what is right and just, whatever the consequences?

2. Did Pilate fall into the trap of choosing the lesser of two evils?

3. Does Luke make the Jewish leaders look as if they are to blame for Jesus' death?

4. Luke seems to show that Jesus' death was not Pilate's fault. Why might he do this?

5. Was Jesus a martyr?

**Summary**

You will now know that the second trial of Jesus before Pilate resulted in a death sentence, although Pilate did not find Jesus guilty of any charge. A number of people could have been responsible for Jesus' death.

# The crucifixion (1)

## ■ Jesus dies on the cross

> " *As they led him away, they seized Simon from Cyrene, who was on his way in from the country, and put the cross on him and made him carry it behind Jesus. …*
>
> *Two other men, both criminals, were also led out with him to be executed. When they came to the place called the Skull, there they crucified him, along with the criminals – one on his right, the other on his left. Jesus said, 'Father, forgive them, for they do not know what they are doing.' And they divided up his clothes by casting lots. The people stood watching, and the rulers even sneered at him. They said, 'He saved others; let him save himself if he is the Christ of God, the Chosen One.'*
>
> *The soldiers also came up and mocked him. They offered him wine vinegar and said, 'If you are the king of the Jews, save yourself.'*
>
> *There was a written notice above him, which read: THIS IS THE KING OF THE JEWS.*
>
> *One of the criminals who hung there hurled insults at him: 'Aren't you the Christ? Save yourself and us!'*
>
> *But the other criminal rebuked him. 'Don't you fear God,' he said, 'since you are under the same sentence? We are punished justly, for we are getting what our deeds deserve. But this man has done nothing wrong.'*
>
> *Then he said, 'Jesus, remember me when you come into your kingdom.'*
>
> *Jesus answered him, 'I tell you the truth, today you will be with me in paradise.'*
>
> *It was now about the sixth hour, and darkness came over the whole land until the ninth hour, for the sun stopped shining. And the curtain of the temple was torn in two. Jesus called out with a loud voice, 'Father, into your hands I commit my spirit.' When he had said this, he breathed his last.*
>
> *The centurion, seeing what had happened, praised God and said, 'Surely this was a righteous man.' When all the people who had gathered to witness this sight saw what took place, they beat their breasts and went away. But all those who knew him, including the women who had followed him from Galilee, stood at a distance, watching these things.* "
>
> *Luke* 23:26,32–49

**Beliefs and teachings**

Christians believe that Jesus died once for all people and all time, and this is all that is necessary for forgiveness if people accept it.

### Simon of Cyrene

It is not clear why Jesus did not carry his own cross, as was usual for a condemned man. The soldiers made Simon of Cyrene (a place in North Africa) carry the cross instead. Simon had probably just arrived in Jerusalem for the Passover festival. He may have been a follower of Jesus or he may not have joined the Christian community until after this incident. Simon is a good example of discipleship, because although he was forced into carrying the cross he was willing to do so and suffer for Jesus.

∞ links

Discipleship is a key part of Luke's Gospel. See Chapter 6.

## Crucifixion

- **Crucifixion** was a punishment the Romans used for those who rebelled against them. The feet appeared to have been held by one nail, and the arms by a nail each, through the wrist, in order to take the weight of the body. In artistic depictions of the crucifixion, however, the nails are almost invariably shown through the palms of Jesus' hands.

- The punishment was cruel because death came slowly, and the victim could be left for days to die. However, in some cases the legs of the victim were broken so that they would suffocate and die more quickly.

**A**   *In Luke's account of the crucifixion, two criminals were crucified with Jesus*

## Jesus' forgiveness

The pain and distress caused by crucifixion is unimaginable, but Luke is clear that Jesus forgave those who had crucified him. The early Christians who were being persecuted could have seen this as an example to show that they should forgive those who were persecuting them. Christians are expected to forgive those who wrong them.

## The crowd's reaction

The crowd were abusive. They used the messianic claim against Jesus, and wanted to see a miracle. Jesus was expected to come down off the cross. The crowd did not understand that Jesus' death was part of God's plan to bring humans and God together again. Jesus was being sacrificed to replace all the blood sacrifices that the Jews had been doing in the Temple.

## The criminals

The two criminals crucified with Jesus reacted very differently. The first one spoke in a selfish way and expected Jesus to save them. The second, however, seemed to show understanding that Jesus' death meant something very different. He would have been reassured by the promise Jesus made that he would see him in paradise.

**Discussion activity**

The death of Jesus makes him a mediator (go-between) between God and humans. Discuss in class what this means.

**Activities**

1. Some people have suggested that Jesus' prayer of forgiveness for those who were crucifying him was added later. If it was, what was the author trying to show about Jesus?

2. What example does Simon of Cyrene set for Christians?

3. What do you think Christians mean by 'Jesus died for our sins'?

4. 'If Jesus had not died Christianity would never have begun.' Do you agree? Give reasons for your answer.

**Summary**

You will now know that Luke's account of the crucifixion includes Simon of Gyrene carrying the cross for Jesus and the reactions of the criminals crucified with him.

## The women

The text informs us that the women had travelled from Galilee to see the events at the end of Jesus' life. This is very typical of Luke. He wanted to show that women were at the centre of Jesus' teaching and activity.

The women here are not named but the other gospel narratives indicate that they included Mary his mother and Mary Magdalene.

Luke does not indicate that the disciples were present at the crucifixion. Following Jesus' arrest many of them may have been frightened that if they appeared in public they too might be arrested.

## The centurion

The **centurion** would not have been Jewish, but he recognised that Jesus was special. He praised God – it would have been very unusual for a Roman to praise the Jewish God in this way. He then described Jesus as 'a righteous man' (Luke 23:47). The centurion regarded Jesus as innocent and is another example of Luke using a positive image of a Gentile reaction. It is another example of Luke's desire to show that Jesus had come for all – not just for the Jews.

**Objectives**

Learn more of the event of the crucifixion.

Note the importance of women and of the centurion in the narrative.

**Key terms**

**Centurion**: an important officer in the Roman Army. A centurion was present at Jesus' crucifixion.

**A** *Via Dolorosa – the street along which Jesus would have travelled on his way to the crucifixion*

**Discussion activity**

The death penalty was very common in Jesus' day. Do you think it is a punishment that should be used today?

## ■ Key points about the crucifixion

### Jesus

- Jesus was crucified as a common criminal.
- Jesus asked God to forgive those who were crucifying him.
- Jesus prayed as he commended his spirit to God.
- Jesus died. This meant that there would be no need for further animal sacrifices to God.

### The crucifixion

- The place of the crucifixion was known as the 'Skull'.
- The inscription on the cross is often depicted in art as 'INRI' – the Latin abbreviation for 'Jesus of Nazareth, King of the Jews'.
- Dividing garments and distributing them among the crowd was a common action at crucifixions.

### Others present at the crucifixion

- Jesus was mocked by the crowd and the soldiers.
- One of the criminals asked, 'Are you not the Christ?' in the hope of being saved.
- The other criminal understood the power of Jesus and was assured of a place in paradise.
- The crowd 'beat their breasts', which is normally a sign of sadness and lamentation.
- Luke states that the women were witnesses to the crucifixion.

**B** *Crucifixion of Jesus*

### Events linked to the crucifixion

- The darkness that fell could symbolise a sense of spiritual darkness – Jesus is dying; his light is going out.
- The Curtain of the Temple Sanctuary was torn in two. The barrier between God and humans, caused by sin, has gone.

Luke's account of the crucifixion shows the importance of the women and the centurion. It also presented a message about the meaning of the crucifixion for Christians and model of forgiveness.

---

**Extension activity**

Compare Psalm 28 with the narrative of the crucifixion in Luke.

---

AQA   **Examiner's tip**

You may be asked whether the crucifixion or the Resurrection is the more important event.

---

**Summary**

You should now understand that Luke's account of the crucifixion shows the importance of the women and the centurion. It also provides a message about the meaning of the crucifixion for Christians.

---

**Activities**

1. How did the women show their loyalty to Jesus at this time?
2. Why was it important for Luke to include what the centurion said?
3. How did Jesus show that he felt God was still with him on the cross?
4. What is the importance of the curtain in the Temple being torn in two?
5. Explain the importance of 'darkness' in the crucifixion narrative.

# 4.8 | The burial

Now there was a man named Joseph, a member of the Council, a good and upright man, who had not consented to their decision and action. He came from the Judean town of Arimathea and he was waiting for the kingdom of God. Going to Pilate, he asked for Jesus' body. Then he took it down, wrapped it in linen cloth and placed it in a tomb cut in the rock, one in which no one had yet been laid. It was Preparation Day, and the Sabbath was about to begin.

The women who had come with Jesus from Galilee followed Joseph and saw the tomb and how his body was laid in it. Then they went home and prepared spices and perfumes. But they rested on the Sabbath in obedience to the commandment.

*Luke* 23:50-56

## Objectives

Know Luke's account of the burial of Jesus.

Learn what is known about Joseph of Arimathea.

Understand the importance of the crucifixion for Christians.

**A** *The traditional site of the burial of Jesus*

## Joseph of Arimathea

Arimathea was a small town in Judea; its location is not known for certain. Joseph is described as a 'member of the Council', which means that he could have been one of Jesus' enemies. However, he had nothing to do with the trials and crucifixion.

Joseph owned an unused tomb in Jerusalem, probably ready for his own burial. Rich people did not expect to be buried in common graves with the poor.

Joseph became a focus of legend. It was told that he collected some of Jesus' blood and sweat from the crucifixion and travelled though France to Glastonbury in Somerset. There a holy thorn, which flowers at Christmas, is said to have grown from his staff, which he planted in the ground.

## Research activity

Look up the legends of Joseph of Arimathea. They give a good idea of the way in which the legends and stories of the followers of Jesus developed.

## ■ The burial

It was evening on Friday, and the burial was hurried because of the Sabbath. The Jewish Sabbath begins at sunset on Friday. There was no time to put spices on the body.

The presence of the women is emphasised in the burial, partly because it would have been their role to clean the body and anoint it with spices, but also because of what follows in the narrative. For Luke and for Christian believers, two things are essential in the crucifixion and burial story:

- Jesus was truly dead.
- The women knew exactly where the tomb was in which Jesus had been buried.

## ■ The importance of the Passion and death of Jesus

Christians believe that the crucifixion and resurrection were all part of God's plan. Even though Jesus does not seem to have had a fair trial, he did not try to escape and did not really try to defend himself.

Jesus went to Jerusalem knowing what would happen. He knew he had a destiny, and he knew also that he would rise again.

Christians believe that Jesus wanted to:

- set an example of true discipleship to God by suffering without complaint for his beliefs
- offer himself as a once and for all sacrifice. He would bring people back to a relationship with God, with their sins forgiven. People would no longer have to face punishment after death, if they repented
- fulfil the prophecies in the Old Testament that the Messiah would suffer and die.

In order for slaves to be freed in the ancient world, they had to be 'redeemed'. A sum of money would be paid to their master to free them. Jesus was doing something similar: redeeming the people from the sins that had enslaved them. He was freeing the people so that they could get close to God.

**Activities**

1  Why was the burial hurried?
2  What was the role of the women at this stage of the narrative?
3  Why was it important to Luke to emphasise that Jesus was dead and that the women knew exactly where the tomb was?
4  Look up I Corinthians 15:1–5,12–14. Paul is clearly answering those who had doubts about the resurrection. What does he confirm about Jesus' death and burial?

**Summary**

Your will now know that Jesus was buried in a borrowed tomb and in a hurried manner on the Friday evening. Christians believe Jesus really died and that his death enabled people to get close to God.

## The empty tomb

> ❝ On the first day of the week, very early in the morning, the women took the spices they had prepared and went to the tomb. They found the stone rolled away from the tomb, but when they entered, they did not find the body of the Lord Jesus. While they were wondering about this, suddenly two men in clothes that gleamed like lightning stood beside them. In their fright the women bowed down with their faces to the ground, but the men said to them, 'Why do you look for the living among the dead? He is not here; he has risen! Remember how he told you, while he was still with you in Galilee: "The Son of Man must be delivered into the hands of sinful men, be crucified and on the third day be raised again." ' Then they remembered his words. When they came back from the tomb, they told all these things to the Eleven and to all the others. It was Mary Magdalene, Joanna, Mary the mother of James, and the others with them who told this to the apostles. But they did not believe the women, because their words seemed to them like nonsense. Peter, however, got up and ran to the tomb. Bending over, he saw the strips of linen lying by themselves, and he went away, wondering to himself what had happened. ❞
>
> *Luke* 24:1–12

Jesus had predicted that he would die and rise again. Luke, the historian, wanted identifiable witnesses. Women were not regarded as good witnesses, so it was important that Peter checked and was able to verify what they had seen.

The disciples did not believe the women so Peter ran off to the tomb and saw nothing but the linen strips.

## Did Jesus rise from the dead?

This is a very old debate. There are two main points of view.

**Jesus rose:**

- The women witnessed the empty tomb.
- Peter also saw the tomb empty.
- There were later sightings of Jesus (see pages 96–97).
- The tomb became unimportant and certainly was not a place of pilgrimage.
- Christians were tortured and killed for claiming that Jesus rose, and it is unlikely that they would have done this for something that was made up.
- The **resurrection** completes Jesus' teaching and proves that he was the Son of God.
- The resurrection proves God's plan that Jesus has brought a new relationship and a new covenant (see pages 78–79) into being.

### Objectives

Study Luke's account of the resurrection.

Know and understand the role of the women and Peter in the narrative.

Consider the debate that surrounds the resurrection.

### ⚭ links

The women were terrified by the angels. Look at pages 38–39 and 46–47 to see Mary's reaction and the shepherds' reaction to angels.

### Beliefs and teachings

Christians believe that Jesus rose from the dead.

### AQA Examiner's tip

It is worth knowing these arguments as well as having your own views and arguments to support them.

### Key terms

**The resurrection**: when Jesus rose from the dead after dying on the cross. One of the key beliefs of Christianity.

## Jesus' body was stolen:

Rumours began after Jesus' death that he had not risen from the dead, and the body had been stolen. Who could have done this?

### The disciples

Jesus had been arrested, tortured and crucified, and was buried. The disciples did not know who would be arrested next, and it was the Sabbath. It is not very likely that they would steal a body and dispose of it. Later, the disciples were arrested and tortured but they persisted in preaching that Jesus had risen (Acts 2).

### The Jewish authorities

The authorities could have taken the body. If they had produced the body later, they would perhaps have silenced the message that Jesus had risen from the dead. The authorities never produced the body, and there is no evidence that they took it.

### The Romans

As far as the Romans were concerned, Jesus was an insignificant leader of an insignificant group of Galileans whom the Jewish authorities wanted dead. There was no reason for the Romans to take the body.

**A**   *The entrance to the garden tomb*

## Other possibilities:

### The women went to the wrong tomb

Luke emphasised that the women had witnessed the crucifixion. They had then gone to the tomb and seen Joseph arrange the burial. Within 36 hours they returned to the tomb to anoint the body of Jesus.

### They were hallucinating

This has been put forward as a theory. Indeed, the disciples may have thought this at first when the women claimed that the tomb was empty. However, other people also claimed that they saw Jesus after the resurrection.

### Jesus did not die

Jesus could have been taken from the cross before he died. He might then have recovered in the coolness of the tomb. How could he have suffered so much and survived? How could he get out of a sealed tomb?

### It was not a bodily resurrection

The disciples saw a ghost. In Luke's account of the post-resurrection appearances, however, Jesus walks and talks, and then breaks bread physically. He is recognised as a person.

### Summary

You will now know Luke's account of the resurrection of Jesus and some of the debates around it.

# 4.10 The Emmaus Road appearance

## On the road to Emmaus

> *Now that same day two of them were going to a village called Emmaus, about seven miles from Jerusalem. They were talking with each other about everything that had happened. As they talked and discussed these things with each other, Jesus himself came up and walked along with them; but they were kept from recognising him. He asked them, 'What are you discussing together as you walk along?' They stood still, their faces downcast. One of them, named Cleopas, asked him, 'Are you only a visitor to Jerusalem and do not know the things that have happened there in these days?'*
>
> *'What things?' he asked.*
>
> *'About Jesus of Nazareth,' they replied. 'He was a prophet, powerful in word and deed before God and all the people. The chief priests and our rulers handed him over to be sentenced to death, and they crucified him; but we had hoped that he was the one who was going to redeem Israel. And what is more, it is the third day since all this took place. In addition, some of our women amazed us. They went to the tomb early this morning but didn't find his body. They came and told us that they had seen a vision of angels, who said he was alive. Then some of our companions went to the tomb and found it just as the women had said, but him they did not see.'*
>
> *He said to them, 'How foolish you are, and how slow of heart to believe all that the prophets have spoken! Did not the Christ have to suffer these things and then enter his glory?' And beginning with Moses and all the Prophets, he explained to them what was said in all the Scriptures concerning himself.*
>
> *As they approached the village to which they were going, Jesus acted as if he were going farther. But they urged him strongly, 'Stay with us, for it is nearly evening; the day is almost over.' So he went in to stay with them. When he was at the table with them, he took bread, gave thanks, broke it and began to give it to them. Then their eyes were opened and they recognized him, and he disappeared from their sight. They asked each other, 'Were not our hearts burning within us while he talked with us on the road and opened the Scriptures to us?'*
>
> *They got up and returned at once to Jerusalem. There they found the Eleven and those with them, assembled together and saying, 'It is true! The Lord has risen and has appeared to Simon.' Then the two told what had happened on the way, and how Jesus was recognised by them when he broke the bread.*
>
> *Luke* 24:13–35

### Objectives

Learn about the Emmaus Road resurrection appearance.

Understand how it shows Jesus as the Messiah.

Think about how it might support Christians in difficulty.

Have you ever seen someone you know, but not where you expected to see him or her, and so not recognised them? This is what happened to the disciples. This story is only in Luke's Gospel.

The story of the two disciples on the road to Emmaus captures the essence of Luke's Gospel. These disciples were not important people. One is called Cleopas. The other is not named and at least one

**A** *Artist's impression of the road to Emmaus*

commentator has suggested that it could have been Cleopas' wife. It is a characteristic of Luke to include this account in his gospel, because for him it is significant that the risen Jesus appeared to unknown disciples, not just well-known people.

The teaching in the passage is very important. As Jesus spoke with the disciples, he emphasised the links back to the Old Testament. Cleopas had hoped that Jesus would free Israel, but this now seemed impossible.

### Life after death

The two disciples were very downhearted because Jesus had been crucified. Then they heard that he had risen from the dead, so they must have been very confused too. In this story there is no doubt that Jesus rose again. When Christians face difficult times, this promise of life after death gives them hope.

## ■ The breaking of bread

Jesus stayed with the travellers and revealed himself by re-enacting what happened at the Last Supper. At once, they recognised him through his actions.

Some people have questioned whether these actions were a reference to the Last Supper at all, as it is normal Jewish practice to bless and break bread. However, the breaking of bread had another possible importance.

Jesus was overturning the old relationship with God, and the meal – the first after the Resurrection – overturned the effect of Adam and Eve eating the fruit that broke the link with God. This new 'breaking of bread' is a sign to Christians that the relationship with God is restored.

## ■ The reaction

The two disciples remembered how they had felt when Jesus was speaking to them, and their hearts were 'burning' within them. It would have been dark and dangerous on the road, but they were so excited that they went straight to Jerusalem to tell the others what had happened, and most importantly how they had recognised Jesus.

Christians often say they feel a real sense of exhilaration and excitement when talking of Jesus. This is a form of inspiration, and is a **religious experience** for many. Some Christians are convinced that God or Jesus has spoken to them directly.

Christians are encouraged by this story because:

- it is proof that Jesus was alive on that Sunday
- it gives a promise of life after death
- it gave strength to early disciples to keep believing in what must have seemed impossible
- it gave the disciples inspiration
- Jesus joined the two disciples, and Christians believe that he is with disciples today.

**B** *They recognised Jesus as he broke bread*

**Activities**

1  After what had happened to Jesus, were Cleopas and his companion wise to speak with the stranger about Jesus?

2  What did Jesus do to help them recognise him?

3  Why would this make it difficult to say, as some do, that Jesus was a ghost?

4  How would this story help Christians facing danger?

5  If someone you knew claimed that Jesus or God had spoken directly to him or her what would your reaction be?

**Summary**

You will now know Luke's account of Jesus' appearance to two people travelling to Emmaus and how they eventually recognised him through the breaking of bread. The resurrection gave great hope to early Christians, and Christians today still believe Jesus is present with them.

# 4.11 Why is the resurrection important to Christians?

## A holy day

The fact that the Christian holy day is Sunday emphasises the importance of the resurrection. The earliest Christians were all Jewish, but they left behind the Jewish Sabbath, which was from sunset on Friday to sunset on Saturday, and began to worship on Sunday. This is because they believe the tomb was empty and that God had raised Jesus from the dead on a Sunday.

### The resurrection gives Christians faith

- Jesus did not die as a punishment – he died to bring people back to a good relationship with God.
- Christianity is the only religion based on the founder rising from the dead. It gives it a unique characteristic – the founder is still alive.
- Christians can feel that they are praying to a living person and that their prayers will therefore be heard.
- They are certain that there is the promise of life after death: if Jesus rose from the dead then so will they. This belief is a major part of Christian funeral services.

### The resurrection gives Christians strength

- Christians believe that they are called to change the world and they rely on their faith in the resurrection to give them the strength to do this.
- They are encouraged to try to create the Kingdom of God, with its emphasis on justice and equality.
- People change their whole way of life as a result of their belief in Jesus and the resurrection. An example of this is Nicky Cruz (who became Christian having been in the gangs of New York).

### Oscar Romero

Many Christian martyrs are prepared to die for their belief. An example is Oscar Romero, who died at the altar of his cathedral in El Salvador in 1980.

He believed that his death would bring eternal life, and was determined to oppose the government of the time.

### The resurrection gives Christians hope

- Christians believe that they will one day be with Jesus in the Kingdom of God. In the Apostles Creed they state that they believe in 'the resurrection of the body'.
- The resurrection is about new life. Paul states in his writing, 'I no longer live, but Christ lives in me.' (Galatians 2:20) Christians want to bring that new life to those in need.

**A**  Oscar Romero

- It encouraged the early Christians to challenge their society and modern believers to do the same.
- Christians believe that they will have eternal life.

### Bringing hope to others

Christians also believe that they should use their sense of hope to bring hope to others. This is the motivation of some of the organisations that you have studied such as Christian Aid and CAFOD.

In this case the hope they bring is not just some idea of life after death but a real change to the daily lives of the people in the world today.

---

### Oscar Romero

Case study

Oscar Romero was the Archbishop of El Salvador in Central America.  He was shot dead by government troops on 23 March 1980 while celebrating mass. He had opposed government corruption for some years and knew that his life was in danger. This did not stop him standing up for his beliefs. Oscar Romero believed that he was called to serve God and share the Christian message, and he said that he did not fear persecution so long as he was working for the rights of the poor. After his death it is reported that over 100,000 Christians and others (including rebels) joined together to demand a more democratic government.

*www.romerotrust.org.uk*

---

**B**  *San Salvador Cathedral*

---

**Discussion activity**

Consider this Christian Aid slogan:

'We believe in life before death.'

What do you think of it?

**Beliefs and teachings**

Should Christians be actively engaged in politics?

---

**Activities**

1. Would the Christian religion have survived if Jesus had not risen from the dead?
2. Is the resurrection the most important part of the Christian faith?
3. How would the resurrection bring hope to Christians?
4. What do Christians believe about life after death?
5. The empty cross is the most important symbol of Christianity. Do you agree? Give reasons for your answer.

---

**Summary**

You will now understand that the resurrection is central to the Christian faith. It has provided strength, hope and encouragement for Christians, especially in times of persecution or difficulty.

**4**

## The suffering, death and resurrection of Jesus – summary

For the examination you should now be able to:

✔ describe Luke's account of
  - the Last Supper
  - Jesus on the Mount of Olives
  - The trials of Jesus
  - The crucifixion
  - The resurrection appearances

✔ explain the importance of the suffering, death and resurrection for Jesus, for those personally involved at the time and for Christians today.

### Sample answer

**1** Write an answer to the following examination question:

'The crucifixion of Jesus is more important than the resurrection.' Do you agree? Give reasons for your answer, showing that you have thought about more than one point of view. *(6 marks)*

**2** Read the following sample answer.

> 'Some Christians believe that the crucifixion of Jesus is more important than the Resurrection because in the crucifixion Jesus dies for our sins. In dying he is like a sacrifice and without that, God would still be a distant thing to us. We would not be able to do enough good things to satisfy God. However, Jesus allows us to be forgiven by God if we ask for it because he died. Other Christians do not agree. They believe that the resurrection is more important because it proves that Jesus is the Messiah. If the resurrection had not happened Jesus would still be in the grave and the powers he was supposed to have would not have been proved. Because Jesus rose from the dead he proved that he was the Messiah and that his teachings are worth following. Christianity would never have survived if Jesus had not risen from the dead.'

**3** With a partner, discuss the sample answer. Do you think there are other things that the student could have included in the answer?

**4** What mark would you give this answer out of 6? Look at the mark scheme in the Introduction on page 7 (AO2). What are the reasons for the mark you have given?

# AQA Examination-style questions

Look at this picture and answer the following questions

**1** Give a detailed account of the Last Supper. *(6 marks)*

**2** Describe in detail the trial before the Jewish council. *(6 marks)*

**3** Give a detailed account of the conversation between Jesus and the criminals at the crucifixion. *(6 marks)*

**4** Give a detailed account of the resurrection of Jesus. *(6 marks)*

**5** 'Pilate should have done his duty.' Do you agree? Give reasons for your answer, showing that you have thought about more than one point of view. *(6 marks)*

**6** What part did the Roman soldiers play in Jesus' crucifixion? *(4 marks)*

**7** 'The resurrection never happened. It is impossible.' Do you agree? Give reasons for your answer showing that you have thought about more than one point of view. *(6 marks)*

**8** How would persecuted Christians be helped by the death and resurrection of Jesus? *(6 marks)*

**9** Why did Luke include resurrection appearances at the end of his Gospel? *(6 marks)*

## 5.1 Jesus the Messiah for all people

### ▮ Outsiders and outcasts

In Luke there is clear evidence that Jesus supported and encouraged those on the fringes of Jewish society, such as tax collectors, Samaritans, Gentiles, Romans and women. Luke included stories about these groups to emphasise Jesus' belief that all could enter the kingdom of heaven.

**Universalism** is an idea that goes back to the Old Testament.

The symbol for Luke is traditionally the ox. This seems appropriate for a gospel writer who showed Jesus to have supported those in society who had the greatest burdens to bear.

**Objectives**

Learn about some of the groups on the fringes of Jewish society.

Understand that Jesus saw himself as a universal Messiah for all people.

**Key terms**

**Universalism**: a central theme in Luke's Gospel, it refers to Jesus' acceptance of everyone, including those despised and looked down on by most people.

**AQA  Examiner's tip**

You may be asked a question about Jesus' attitude to those on the fringes of Jewish society.

**A**  *Luke depicted as a winged ox*

### Tax collectors

Tax collectors were hated by the Jews. They worked for the Romans and collected taxes that most Jews believed they should not have to pay. The tax collectors were also often dishonest. Jesus had no hesitation in challenging them, with the hope of transforming their lives.

**∞ links**

The shepherds were also a group outside society, but they were important in the birth stories described. See Chapter 2.

**∞ links**

Read the story of Zacchaeus, a tax collector, on pages 114–115.

## Samaritans

The Samaritans split from the Jews in about the 4th century BCE. They believed that they kept the commandments of the Law more strictly than the Jews, and that their sanctuary on Mount Gerizim was older and therefore more important that Jerusalem. They shared some of the same scriptures as the Jews. They were so hated that Galilean pilgrims going to Jerusalem would not pass though Samaritan country. The Samaritans still exist today as an identifiable group near the modern city of Nablus in Israel.

Jesus praised Samaritans on two occasions. Once was in the Parable of the Good Samaritan (see pages 110–111). The other time was after Jesus healed ten lepers: nine were Jews and one was a Samaritan, and only the Samaritan came back to thank him (Luke 17:15–18). Samaritans suffered prejudice and discrimination from some Jewish people and this incident would have challenged the Jewish view.

## Gentiles

Gentiles are non-Jewish people. Because they had the Covenant, the Jews regarded themselves as a chosen people: Gentiles could not be part of this Covenant. The Romans were not only outside Jewish society because they were Gentiles, but were hated as the occupying power. Jesus treated Gentiles just as he would any other people.

In the birth stories Jesus was described by Simeon as 'a light for revelation to the Gentiles' (Luke 2:32). After the resurrection, Jesus told his disciples that 'repentance and forgiveness of sins will be preached in his name to all nations, beginning at Jerusalem' (Luke 24:47).

## Women

Women in 1st-century Palestine were regarded as the property of their husbands. Their place was in the home doing domestic work and bringing up the children. Women could not give evidence, they could not speak to strangers in public and were expected to be veiled in public. They could not teach.

Women were kept outside the religious practices of the day. They could not be priests, and sat separately from the men in the synagogue.

Luke mentions 13 women who do not appear in any of the other gospels. He relates the incident concerning the widow of Nain (see pages 106–107), who was not only a woman but also a Gentile.

Jesus' attitude was revolutionary. He would speak to women in public and treat them with respect, and taught women alongside men. Women belonged to the wider group of the disciples.

Women are very important in the birth stories and at the crucifixion and resurrection of Jesus.

### Summary

You will now know that Luke has a theme of universalism running through his Gospel. He portrays Jesus as the Messiah for all people, especially those on the fringes of society.

### Extension activity

1 Read Luke 9:52–56. What does this show about the attitude of some of Jesus' disciples towards the Samaritans?

### Extension activity

2 Find out about the work of those such as the Connection at St Martin in the Fields, London (www.connection-at-stmartins.org.uk), who work with people on the fringes of society today. Find out about local organisations that do similar work in your area. Invite a speaker in or visit the organisation if possible.

### Activities

1 Which groups did Jesus show a special interest in and why do you think this was?

2 What does Jesus' dealings with these groups teach about the Messiah?

3 Why would some Jews have a problem with Jesus' teaching on universalism?

4 How can Christians use Jesus' teaching and example to help people who are on the fringes of society today?

# 5.2    The centurion's servant

## ■ The centurion's faith

> **❝** *Jesus … entered Capernaum. There a centurion's servant, whom his master valued highly, was sick and about to die. The centurion heard of Jesus and sent some elders of the Jews to him, asking him to come and heal his servant. When they came to Jesus, they pleaded earnestly with him, 'This man deserves to have you do this, because he loves our nation and has built our synagogue.' So Jesus went with them.*
>
> *He was not far from the house when the centurion sent friends to say to him: 'Lord, don't trouble yourself, for I do not deserve to have you come under my roof. That is why I did not even consider myself worthy to come to you. But say the word, and my servant will be healed. For I myself am a man under authority, with soldiers under me. I tell this one, "Go," and he goes; and that one, "Come," and he comes. I say to my servant, "Do this," and he does it.' When Jesus heard this, he was amazed at him, and turning to the crowd following him, he said, 'I tell you, I have not found such great faith even in Israel.' Then the men who had been sent returned to the house and found the servant well.* **❞**
>
> *Luke* 7:1–10

This narrative is an account of a miracle in which Jesus did not meet the ill person or even the person with the faith to enable the healing to take place. The event is important because of the people involved and Jesus' response to them.

Jesus showed his belief in the **equality** of all human beings and the importance of not being prejudiced against individuals.

### A Roman centurion

The Romans were an occupying force in 1st-century Palestine. They were tolerant of the Jewish religion but were still regarded by many as the enemy. It was not uncommon for Roman soldiers to adopt the local religion where they were stationed.

This Roman centurion clearly got on well with the local community in Capernaum. He was able to send some of the Jewish elders to Jesus to ask him for help. The leaders asked Jesus to help the centurion because, they said, 'he built our synagogue'.

The centurion had so much respect for Jesus that he did not feel it was his place to request help, or perhaps, as a Gentile, he expected **discrimination** or rejection. He may have thought Jesus would be more likely to help him if Jewish people asked.

Jesus did not hesitate to go to meet a need. It did not matter that it was a Roman that was asking for help, nor did it matter that the centurion did not ask himself. The centurion had faith.

---

**Objectives**

Study the incident of the centurion's servant.

Understand that Jesus was prepared to help anyone in need, whatever their rank or background.

Understand how this incident demonstrates God's power extending to all people, without discrimination.

---

**Key terms**

**Equality**: treating every person in a way that ensures justice and fairness.

**Discrimination**: to treat someone or something differently either favouring or denying something, e.g. not allowing lepers to be part of the community.

---

**AQA**   **Examiner's tip**

You will need to be able to remember this story accurately as well as be able to draw conclusions from it.

**A**   *A Roman centurion*

**Research activity**

Do a web search on charities who help asylum seekers in the UK. Are they fulfilling Jesus' teaching?

### 'I do not deserve to have you come under my roof'

The centurion clearly felt humble. He recognised that Jesus was a man of some importance. He explained, through friends, that he did not feel worthy to contact Jesus himself.

His faith then came out in a very real way. As a Roman officer he was used to commanding men and having them obey. He recognised a similar authority in Jesus. Jesus only had to say the word, and the servant would be healed.

### 'Jesus ... was amazed'

It is characteristic of Luke that he emphasises that the centurion who had such a strong faith was a Gentile. Jesus did not miss the opportunity to tell the crowd what he thought about the centurion's faith. He said that he had not seen so much faith as this among the Jews.

The messengers went home and found the servant recovered from his illness, showing Jesus' power as a miracle worker. This power is recognised by a Gentile who realised that Jesus could help his servant.

**Activities**

1. What happened when the centurion asked Jesus to cure his servant?
2. What does this show about the centurion?
3. What does this narrative demonstrate about Jesus' attitude to those in need?
4. Jesus criticised the Jews in this story. What did he say and what did he mean?
5. How does this story show that Jesus was not prejudiced and did not discriminate against people?

**Summary**

You will now know that Luke records a miracle story involving a Gentile who had faith, a story that shows Jesus was the Messiah for all people and not just for the Jews.

# 5.3    The widow of Nain

## The widow's son

> ❝ Soon afterward, Jesus went to a town called Nain, and his disciples and a large crowd went along with him. As he approached the town gate, a dead person was being carried out – the only son of his mother, and she was a widow. And a large crowd from the town was with her. When the Lord saw her, his heart went out to her and he said, 'Don't cry.' Then he went up and touched the coffin, and those carrying it stood still. He said, 'Young man, I say to you, get up!' The dead man sat up and began to talk, and Jesus gave him back to his mother. They were all filled with awe and praised God. 'A great prophet has appeared among us,' they said. 'God has come to help his people.' This news about Jesus spread throughout Judea and the surrounding country. ❞
>
> *Luke* 7:11–17

**A**    *Son of the widow of Nain*

Nain is thought to be about 25 miles from Capernaum – at least a day's walk, and probably two. Luke records this event happening soon after the healing of the centurion's servant.

This miracle was performed for a woman who would have been in some difficulty. With her son dead, she might have had no one to support her. Jesus saved her from that problem and brought her son back to life.

### Jesus' reaction

Jesus' reaction was to help and comfort the woman. He told her to stop crying, touched the bier, which would have made him unclean, and then told the young man to get up. This command was similar to that given in the healing of the paralysed man.

When the dead man got up and began to talk, the crowd reacted with amazement. They praised God, recognising Jesus as a prophet sent by God.

**Objectives**

Learn about the raising from the dead of the son of the widow of Nain.

Understand that Jesus was prepared to help Gentiles.

Show Jesus sharing God's power with all.

**Key terms**

**Widow:** a woman whose husband had died. In Jesus' time they had little support apart from their family.

∞ **links**

Luke often included women, as we also saw in Mary and Martha (see pages 74–75).

**Discussion activity** 👤👤👤

Are the stories of Jesus raising people from the dead proof of life after death? Discuss what evidence there is, for example, out of body experiences.

∞ **links**

The healing of the paralysed man is discussed on pages 66–67.

## Raising from the dead

There are three miracles in the Gospel that involve Jesus raising someone from the dead:

- the son of the **widow** of Nain in this account
- Jairus' daughter (Luke 8: 40–42, 49–56)
- Lazarus (John 11:1–44).

**B**   *Nain in Isarel*

There does not seem to be much doubt that the son of the widow of Nain was dead – he was being carried away for burial. Jesus was able to bring life from death. For Christians this is a good example of the promise of new life that Christianity brings.

### Activities

1. There is no evidence of faith in this story. What does this teach about Jesus' attitude to those in need?
2. What did Jesus do wrong in this miracle from a Jewish believer's point of view?
3. What does this story teach about Jesus' message and work?
4. How does this story point towards Jesus' own death – what similarities are there?
5. Imagine you were there. Describe the events as if you were telling them to someone else. Include your reaction.

## Elijah and the widow's son

Like the healing of the centurion's servant, this story links back to the Old Testament. In I Kings 17 there is a story similar to that of the widow of Nain. Elijah the prophet brings a widow's son back to life in Zarephath, and we are told Elijah then 'gave him back to his mother'.

In Elijah's case the widow was amazed and in Jesus' case it was the crowd who were amazed. Jesus and Elijah were both seen as demonstrating God's power.

**links**

You can read about the raising of Jairus' daughter on pages 48–49.

AQA   *Examiner's tip*

As well as being able to retell this story, be prepared to emphasise:

- the reaction of the crowd
- the instant effect of Jesus' actions and words
- the importance of the fact that the person Jesus helped was a woman and a Gentile.

**Summary**

You will now know Luke's account of an incident when Jesus saw the need of a woman who was a Gentile and, without being asked, demonstrated God's power.

### ■ Jesus' teaching methods

#### Parables

One of the main ways in which Jesus tried to put across his message about the Kingdom of God was through parables. These are stories with themes taken from everyday life. Jesus used them to get his hearers to think about his message. In many cases they are very simple stories, and every generation needs to interpret them.

#### Why use parables?

- Parables were a well-established teaching approach among the Pharisees, so people were used to hearing them.
- Parables were drawn from everyday situations that people would identify with.
- Much of Jesus' teaching was done in the open to crowds and smaller groups. Parables were easy for listeners to take in and remember and could be dramatic.
- Because the stories took their themes from everyday life, people could feel that a parable was aimed at them – even if it did not mention them by name or by group.
- Parables could be interpreted in different ways so the hearers could draw their own conclusions and make the meaning personal.
- Parables made people think about their own beliefs and attitudes.
- Parables might be made-up stories but they had a truth behind them for people to learn.
- It was easier to teach about God and what God required of people through story, rather than using deep theology.
- Strong messages could be given through parables and people's prejudices could be challenged.
- Parables often gave the opportunity for people to ask questions for greater guidance and understanding of Jesus' message.
- Parables can stand the test of time – although told in one place at a specific time, they can have universal meaning and importance.

**A** *Stories are a very powerful teaching tool*

**B** *Jesus taught in parables – an artist's depiction of the lost son*

## Interpreting the parables

Understanding the parables sometimes means interpreting them and teasing out the meaning. There are several ways of interpreting the parables of Jesus:

- **Allegorical.** An allegorical interpretation involves changing the elements of the parable into something else. Some ancient writers thought this was the only way to interpret every parable. The Parable of the Sower in Luke 8 is an example of a parable that is to be interpreted in this way. Without interpretation, the Parable of the Sower could have left the crowd wondering what it was about.

- **Literal.** In some parables, what Jesus said is what he meant. The Parable of the Lost Sheep (Luke 15:3–6) could have been understood as an instruction to look for lost sheep, and its meaning for the audience would be clear.

- **Metaphorical.** Some parables should be treated as metaphors, where the story is used to help explain a difficult abstract idea. They tell people what the Kingdom of God is *like*... An example of this is the Parable of the Great Banquet (Luke 14:12–24).

Whenever you study a parable, always look at it in context: What was happening at the time? Who was Jesus speaking to? This can help you to understand it.

## Sayings

As you read through Luke's Gospel, you will see some very short sayings in which Jesus gives a teaching point. Some of them are almost like proverbs. An example is, 'He also told them this parable: "Can a blind man lead a blind man? Will they both fall into a pit?"' (Luke 6:39). This word picture offers a clear meaning.

## Direct challenge

Jesus was often asked questions. His answers were sometimes extremely challenging and left the questioner in no doubt what they should do. A good example of this is the question Jesus asked in the story of the rich young ruler.

**Research activity**

Read these parables and analyse how they should be interpreted.

Luke 15:8–10

Luke 19:17–24

Luke 20:9–18.

**AQA**  **Examiner's tip**

You will not be expected to learn these parables.

**⚭ links**

The story of the rich young ruler is discussed on pages 128–129.

**Activities**

1. Explain in your own words at least four reasons why Jesus told parables.
2. Does challenging people always get them to change their beliefs?
3. If Jesus upset people in his teaching and actions, would it make him more or less successful in his work?
4. How can a made-up story contain truth?
5. 'Jesus' parables can have no meaning for today.' What do you think? Give reasons for your answer.

**Summary**

You will now know that Jesus often used parables when he was teaching. The parables could be interpreted in a number of ways, but people found them helpful and memorable.

# The Parable of the Good Samaritan

## A lawyer questions Jesus

> On one occasion an expert in the law stood up to test Jesus. 'Teacher,' he asked, 'what must I do to inherit eternal life?'
>
> 'What is written in the Law?' he replied. 'How do you read it?' He answered: ' 'Love the Lord your God with all your heart and with all your soul and with all your strength and with all your mind,' and, 'Love your neighbour as yourself.'
>
> 'You have answered correctly,' Jesus replied. 'Do this and you will live.' But he wanted to justify himself, so he asked Jesus, 'And who is my neighbour?'
>
> In reply Jesus said: 'A man was going down from Jerusalem to Jericho, when he fell into the hands of robbers. They stripped him of his clothes, beat him and went away, leaving him half dead. A priest happened to be going down the same road, and when he saw the man, he passed by on the other side. So too, a Levite, when he came to the place and saw him, passed by on the other side. But a Samaritan, as he travelled, came where the man was; and when he saw him, he took pity on him. He went to him and bandaged his wounds, pouring on oil and wine. Then he put the man on his own donkey, took him to an inn and took care of him. The next day he took out two silver coins and gave them to the innkeeper. 'Look after him,' he said, 'and when I return, I will reimburse you for any extra expense you may have.'
>
> 'Which of these three do you think was a neighbour to the man who fell into the hands of robbers?'
>
> The expert in the law replied, 'The one who had mercy on him.' Jesus told him, 'Go and do likewise.'
>
> *Luke* 10:25–37

This parable is only found in Luke. It emphasises the way Jesus recognised that foreigners, or Gentiles, were as capable as Jewish people of doing the right thing. Indeed, there is a great challenge to his Jewish hearers in this parable.

## How do I inherit eternal life?

A lawyer at the time of Jesus would have needed an excellent understanding of the Torah. Jesus did not answer the man's question, but instead posed another question.

The man then quoted two Old Testament verses (Deuteronomy 6:5; Leviticus 19:18). Neither quotation is part of the Ten Commandments. However, they cover duty to God and duty to other people.

Jesus' question to the lawyer and his response to the man's answer show that he recognised the value of the Torah. As far as Jesus was concerned, truly keeping these two rules, which summarised the Jewish law, would enable the lawyer to gain eternal life.

### Objectives

Know and understand the parable of the Good Samaritan.

Consider the importance of the parable.

### Key terms

**Samaritans**: the Samaritans were mixed-race Jews. They regarded each other as enemies, so in Luke's Parable of the Good Samaritan, the Samaritan had no obligation to help the injured Jew.

**Prejudice**: to be in favour of, or to be against, someone or something without evidence. To pre-judge.

### AQA Examiner's tip

You will need to be able to retell this story accurately as well as be able to show how it might help Christians to understand their beliefs and the importance of their approach to others.

### Extension activity

Part of Jesus' answer is in the central prayer of the Jews known as the Shema. To examine the Shema in full you need to read Deuteronomy 6:4–9, 11:13–21.

## Who is my neighbour?

The lawyer asked Jesus another question, to gain further understanding and perhaps to test him. In asking, 'Who is my neighbour?' he would have been trying to understand how Jesus regarded different people. Jesus then told the Parable of the Good **Samaritan**.

The importance of Jericho in this story is that it was known as a priestly city. It is estimated that half of the priests lived in Jericho and would travel into Jerusalem for their duties in the Temple.

The parable can be interpreted as a parable against the religious law. If the Priest and the Levite were both going to the Temple to fulfil their rota in the Temple, they would not touch the man in case he was dead. Had they touched him, they would have become ritually unclean.

**A** *The Good Samaritan*

Jesus made the next character in the story a Samaritan. It is conceivable that the crowd's expectation would have been that this person would rob or harm the man. Jesus' story would have shocked them and challenged their **prejudiced**, anti-Samaritan attitudes.

The Samaritan in the story not only helped the injured traveller but went far beyond that. If the man had been dead, the Samaritan would have been made unclean. His compassion overcame this possibility.

## Interpreting the parable

- The parable is a challenge to racist attitudes. With this interpretation it is possible to see how the parable can still have meaning for Christians and others in the world today.
- It could also be a story against the religious laws. The Samaritan did what the priest and the Levite should have done, but did not do because of their strict religious laws. It is all very well to be religious and holy, but if people suffer because of this then it is wrong.
- The parable teaches that people should accept everyone as equal, including those who are hated in society. In answer to the lawyer's question, your 'neighbour' is anyone who is in need of your help.
- The story challenges all believers to make sure that they are not prejudiced and do not discriminate against those on the fringes of society.

## Chad Varah and the Samaritans

In 1953 an Anglican clergyman, Dr Chad Varah, founded the Samaritans after reading of a 13-year-old girl who killed herself. The organisation now has over 200 branches and supports those who feel neglected or in despair. It is known internationally as the Befrienders.

Samaritan volunteers are trained to help all those who contact them. It is not surprising that Chad Varah chose the name 'Samaritans' for the organisation. He said: 'Befriending is fundamental; we must go along beside someone's pain.'

### Summary

You will now know the Parable of the Good Samaritan, which shows Jesus' teaching that all are equal in God's eyes and that prejudice should be challenged. The parable also teaches that a neighbour is anyone in need.

### Extension activity

Do a web search on the work of the Samaritans, **www.samaritans.org**. How do they follow Jesus' example of helping those in need, irrespective of who they are?

### Discussion activity

If everyone followed the commands 'love God' and 'love your neighbour', would we need any other laws? What else would be needed?

### Activities

1. Is it more important to go to church than to help people in need?
2. 'Christians should do more than anyone else to meet the needs of those in trouble.' Do you agree? Give reasons for your answer.
3. Who are the groups that are marginalised today? Make a list and say what could be done to support them.
4. If people always followed the example of the Samaritan in the story, what effect would that have on society?

# 5.6 The Parable of the Lost Son (the Forgiving Father)

## The father's forgiveness

> *Now the tax collectors and 'sinners' were all gathering around to hear him. But the Pharisees and the teachers of the law muttered, 'This man welcomes sinners and eats with them.' ... Jesus continued: 'There was a man who had two sons. The younger one said to his father, "Father, give me my share of the estate." So he divided his property between them. Not long after that, the younger son got together all he had, set off for a distant country and there squandered his wealth in wild living. After he had spent everything, there was a severe famine in that whole country, and he began to be in need. So he went and hired himself out to a citizen of that country, who sent him to his fields to feed pigs. He longed to fill his stomach with the pods that the pigs were eating, but no one gave him anything. When he came to his senses, he said, "How many of my father's hired men have food to spare, and here I am starving to death! I will set out and go back to my father and say to him: Father, I have sinned against heaven and against you. I am no longer worthy to be called your son; make me like one of your hired men." So he got up and went to his father. But while he was still a long way off, his father saw him and was filled with compassion for him; he ran to his son, threw his arms around him and kissed him. The son said to him, "Father, I have sinned against heaven and against you. I am no longer worthy to be called your son." But the father said to his servants, "Quick! Bring the best robe and put it on him. Put a ring on his finger and sandals on his feet. Bring the fattened calf and kill it. Let's have a feast and celebrate. For this son of mine was dead and is alive again; he was lost and is found." So they began to celebrate. Meanwhile, the older son was in the field. When he came near the house, he heard music and dancing. So he called one of the servants and asked him what was going on. "Your brother has come," he replied, "and your father has killed the fattened calf because he has him back safe and sound." The older brother became angry and refused to go in. So his father went out and pleaded with him. But he answered his father, "Look! All these years I've been slaving for you and never disobeyed your orders. Yet you never gave me even a young goat so I could celebrate with my friends. But when this son of yours who has squandered your property with prostitutes comes home, you kill the fattened calf for him!"*
>
> *"My son," the father said, "you are always with me, and everything I have is yours. But we had to celebrate and be glad, because this brother of yours was dead and is alive again; he was lost and is found."'*
>
> *Luke* 15:1–2/11–32

### Objectives

Know and understand the parable of the Lost Son.

Understand the importance of forgiveness.

Understand the image of the Kingdom of God that is in the parable.

### Discussion activity

Analyse the relationship between the father and the two sons. What pressures do families face today?

**A** *What pressures do families face today?*

This is another parable that is only found in Luke. People would have identified easily with this story that describes a family situation, with people making the wrong decisions and the anxiety caused when young people leave home. The parable would have offered the tax collectors and sinners who heard it reassurance of God's love, forgiveness and acceptance.

## The prodigal son

This parable is sometimes referred to as the Prodigal Son. 'Prodigal' is a word for someone who is not at all careful with their possessions.

However, the parable also deals with the relationships between young people and their parents, and the issues that arise in the story are not uncommon today. The son thinks that he knows best, and the father, rather than argue, gives in to him.

This has been described as Jesus' most powerful parable. It is powerful because the son finds himself in a nightmare situation. He loses his money and his 'friends'. For a Jewish young man to have to keep pigs and be tempted to eat what they eat would be a mark of shame and misery. He felt the depths of despair and decides to return home.

## The son returns

The crucial moment in the parable is when the son arrives home and asks for his father's forgiveness. This forgiveness had been given before he arrived, but the son is not to know this.

The father did not even give his son a chance to rehearse the speech he had planned, but immediately gave him the best robe and a ring, and demanded a celebration. The son who was dead was now alive again.

## The brother

The Lost Son's brother was his opposite. He had stayed at home. He was resentful of the father's actions when the Lost Son returned. He did not even go to the house to find out for himself what was happening.

His reaction is negative and he criticised the father from a sense of self-righteousness. He must have looked at his brother and seen how he had upset his father and wasted his inheritance. He would have felt that he had done the right thing himself, yet it was his brother who was rewarded.

He does not even describe him as his brother – when he speaks to his father, he calls him 'this son of yours'.

## ▉ Interpreting the parable

■ The main character is the younger son, the Lost Son. He did things that were wrong and wasted his inheritance. Jesus is taking the opportunity to teach that there is a need for repentance and God's forgiveness will follow, even for the worst sinner.

■ The parable is about the father as much as the sons. His actions of love and forgiveness are like God's actions towards those who sin. This is an example of a parable with an allegorical interpretation.

■ This could be seen as an anti-Pharisee parable. The Pharisees were like the elder brother. They believed that they had kept the Torah, just as the elder brother felt he had been faithful. But the younger son, despite doing what he did, gained the father's forgiveness. Jesus was saying that the Pharisees were like the complaining brother.

■ This is also a parable about resurrection. The father is very clear that his beloved his son was dead and is now alive again.

**B**  *Return of the Prodigal Son by Rembrandt*

## ⚭links

Different ways of interpreting the parables of Jesus' are discussed on pages 108–109.

Different ways of interpreting the parables of Jesus' are discussed on pages 108–109.

### Activities

**1** Why do you think Luke was anxious to emphasise that this parable was told to tax collectors and sinners?

**2** How would this parable have helped the tax collectors and sinners to understand Jesus' message to them?

**3** Are you surprised by any of the father's actions in this story?

**4** The father seems to have given in to the younger son. How important is it for parents to be clear about what they expect in terms of behaviour?

**5** What could Christians learn about the nature of God from the story of the Lost Son?

### Summary

You will now know that the Parable of the Lost Son shows the importance of God's unlimited and unconditional forgiveness. It also demonstrates the acceptance of all who are sorry for what they have done wrong into the Kingdom of God.

# Zacchaeus the tax collector

## Jesus in Jericho

> Jesus entered Jericho and was passing through. A man was there by the name of Zacchaeus; he was a chief tax collector and was wealthy. He wanted to see who Jesus was, but being a short man he could not, because of the crowd. So he ran ahead and climbed a sycamore-fig tree to see him, since Jesus was coming that way. When Jesus reached the spot, he looked up and said to him, 'Zacchaeus, come down immediately. I must stay at your house today.' So he came down at once and welcomed him gladly. All the people saw this and began to mutter, 'He has gone to be the guest of a "sinner".' But Zacchaeus stood up and said to the Lord, 'Look, Lord! Here and now I give half of my possessions to the poor, and if I have cheated anybody out of anything, I will pay back four times the amount.' Jesus said to him, 'Today salvation has come to this house, because this man, too, is a son of Abraham. For the Son of Man came to seek and to save what was lost.'
>
> *Luke* 19:1–10

### Objectives

Learn about the incident of Jesus meeting Zaccheus.

Understand Jesus' attitude to those on the fringes of Jewish society.

See the importance for Christians today.

### AQA Examiner's tip

You will need to able to retell this incident accurately and then show how it adds to Jesus' teaching about who can enter the Kingdom of God.

As a travelling preacher and miracle-worker, Jesus went right though Israel and to the territories around to spread his message. In this incident he is south of Jerusalem, in Jericho. Jericho is important in the history of Israel as the place where Joshua destroyed the walls simply by the people shouting and sounding trumpets (Joshua 6).

Jesus visited this famous city just once, according to Luke. In this incident he demonstrated that he did not accept the prejudices that some people had about the **tax collectors**.

### Key terms

**Tax collectors**: these were despised because they were dishonest, did not keep ritual laws and worked for the Romans.

**Justice**: ensuring that all are treated fairly and their rights are upheld.

## The tax collector

Zacchaeus is described as a chief tax collector. His name means 'righteous one'. Later Jesus described him as a 'Son of Abraham', emphasising that this hated tax collector was just as Jewish as others.

Zacchaeus was so anxious to see Jesus that he climbed a tree to get a good view. So detailed is this story that we know it was a sycamore fig tree.

When Jesus stopped and saw Zacchaeus, he told him to come down and Jesus said to Zacchaeus that he was going to stay in his house. The Greek here says that Jesus actually said, 'I *must* stay at your house today.' Jesus was clearly determined to set an example to the crowd, who would have wanted Jesus to hate the tax collector.

**A** *Tax collectors were despised in the time of Jesus*

**B**  *Zacchaeus climbed a sycamore tree*

## Reactions to Jesus

Luke reported that Zacchaeus received Jesus joyfully. Imagine if someone extremely famous – a person that you were anxious to meet – came to your house! Zacchaeus responded to Jesus by saying that he was going to give half his money to the poor, and that he would repay anyone he had cheated four times the amount out of which he had cheated them.

If you think back to John the Baptist's teaching to the tax collectors, you will remember that he told them to take no more than was due. This is an example of the **justice** for the poor that Jesus was said to bring. In the words that Mary used during her visit to Elizabeth it states, 'He has filled the hungry with good things but has sent the rich away empty' (Luke 1:53).

There is a strong sense of justice about this incident, and a sense of equality. This was the type of change that Jesus wanted. The Kingdom of God would be marked by such changes.

But the crowd were unhappy. How could someone like Jesus go into a tax collector's house? Jesus challenged them. He emphasised that, as a Jewish man, a Son of Abraham, Zacchaeus had been saved and forgiven. Jesus, using the title Son of Man, said, 'The Son of Man came to seek and to save what was lost.'

### Summary

You will now know the story of Zacchaeus was an incident where Jesus treated a tax collector well, and challenged the crowd in doing so.

### Extension activity

How does Zacchaeus compare with the character of Scrooge in Charles Dickens' *A Christmas Carol*?

### Activities

1. How does Luke emphasise how much Jesus was prepared to show that the Kingdom of God was for everyone?

2. Why do you think that Luke includes this narrative in such detail? What are the main teaching points for Christians?

3. Why did the crowd react as they did?

4. How did Zacchaeus demonstrate that he had repented and intended to change?

5. 'Zacchaeus is a good role model for Christians.' Do you agree? Give reasons for your answer.

# 5

## Universalism – summary

For the examination you should be able to:

✔ explain how Jesus took a great interest in marginalised people on the fringes of Jewish society

✔ explain that Jesus taught that the Kingdom of God was for all, and that all were entitled to forgiveness and acceptance

✔ recall and retell the narratives of: the centurion's servant; the widow of Nain; the Parable of the Good Samaritan; the Parable of the Lost Son (Forgiving Father); and the meeting between Jesus and Zacchaeus

✔ understand the significance for Christians of Jesus' attitudes to tax collectors, sinners, non-Jews and women in relation to issues of justice, equality, prejudice and discrimination.

## Sample answer

1. Write an answer to the following examination question:

   'Jesus came to save the lost of Israel.' Do you agree? Give reasons for your answer, showing that you have thought about more than one point of view. *(6 marks)*

2. Read the following sample answer.

'This is not a correct statement. Luke was very keen to show that Jesus came to save everyone from their sins and to change their lives. What is true is that most of his work was with Jewish people. For example in the story of Jairus' daughter Jesus brought her back when the family thought she was dead. Jairus was Jewish. When Jesus met with Zaccheus after he told him to come down from the tree he went to his house for tea. Zacchaeus said that he would repay people that he had cheated (he was a top tax collector) and Jesus called

him a son of Abraham. This means that he was a Jewish man. On the other hand though Jesus was prepared to help those who were not Jewish. He healed the servant of the Roman Centurion. The Roman knew that Jesus was special and so special that he said that he could not have him in his house. Jesus cured the servant even though he never even spoke with the Centurion and said that he had not seen so much faith in Israel. So I disagree with the statement – Jesus came to die for all and save them'

3. With a partner discuss this sample answer. Do you think there are other things that the student could have included in the answer?

4. What mark would you give this out of 6? Look at the mark scheme in the Introduction on page 7 (AO2). What are the reasons for the mark you have given?

# AQA Examination-style questions

 Questions 1–4 are asking you to show that you know and understand specific stories or teaching in Luke. The number of marks given show how much you should be writing in your answer.

**1**   Why were tax collectors hated by many in 1st-century Palestine?   *(3 marks)*

**2**   Why did Zacchaeus climb a tree when Jesus visited Jericho?   *(2 marks)*

**3**   **(i)**   Why was Jesus criticised in the Zacchaeus incident?   *(2 marks)*

    **(ii)**   What was Jesus' reply?   *(3 marks)*

**4**   What can Christians learn about forgiveness from the Parable of the Lost Son?   *(4 marks)*

 Questions 5–7 need you to be able to accurately recall and retell the text.

**5**   Describe in detail the Parable of the Good Samaritan.   *(6 marks)*

**6**   Describe the incident when Jesus raised from the dead the son of a widow in Nain.   *(5 marks)*

**7**   What happened when Jesus went to Jericho and met Zacchaeus?   *(5 marks)*

**8**   'In the Parable of the Lost Son (Forgiving Father), the elder brother spoilt everything.' Do you agree? Give reasons for your answer, showing that you have thought about more than one point of view. (Do **not** retell the parable.)   *(6 marks)*

 In a question like this, which only focuses on one part of a long parable, do not waste time by just retelling the story. Concentrate on the effect of the brother's comments and the conversation that the father had with him.

**9**   How did Luke show that Jesus had come with a message for everyone?   *(6 marks)*

 This type of question allows you to draw from anything in Luke, not just the texts in the specification. Be really careful though that you use only Lukan material – do not use material that is not in Luke, however relevant it seems. You will not get credit for it.

**10**   'Jesus wanted those who heard him to change their way of life.' Do you agree? Give reasons for your answer, showing that you have thought about more than one point of view.   *(6 marks)*

 This needs you to think about the people who heard Jesus and their responses.

## 6.1 The twelve

### The first disciples are called

> One day as Jesus was standing by the Lake of Gennesaret, the people were crowding around him and listening to the word of God. He saw at the water's edge two boats, left there by the fishermen, who were washing their nets. He got into one of the boats, the one belonging to Simon, and asked him to put out a little from shore. Then he sat down and taught the people from the boat. When he had finished speaking, he said to Simon, 'Put out into deep water, and let down the nets for a catch.' Simon answered, 'Master, we've worked hard all night and haven't caught anything. But because you say so, I will let down the nets.'
>
> When they had done so, they caught such a large number of fish that their nets began to break. So they signalled their partners in the other boat to come and help them, and they came and filled both boats so full that they began to sink.
>
> When Simon Peter saw this, he fell at Jesus' knees and said, 'Go away from me, Lord; I am a sinful man!' For he and all his companions were astonished at the catch of fish they had taken, and so were James and John, the sons of Zebedee, Simon's partners.
>
> Then Jesus said to Simon, 'Don't be afraid; from now on you will fish for people.' So they pulled their boats up on shore, left everything and followed him.
>
> *Luke* 5:1–11

Jesus persuaded Simon Peter to allow him to use his boat. Jesus' request for the men to begin fishing met a despairing response at first. But after the catch of fish, Peter recognised that Jesus was a man of power, and used the word 'Lord'. At this point Peter is not recognising Jesus as the Messiah: 'Lord' here simply means 'sir'.

Simon asked Jesus to leave him alone, describing himself as a sinner. The fishermen were amazed at what had happened, and yet again someone had to be told not to be afraid. Jesus then told them that in future their role would be to spread his message and 'fish for people'.

The men called to be the first **disciples** were Simon Peter, and James and John, the sons of Zebedee. It is assumed that Andrew, Simon's brother, was there as well but he is not mentioned. The response of the disciples is instant – they seem to have left everything behind without hesitation.

### The twelve

Jesus went on to call others to be disciples. One of these, Levi, was collecting taxes when he is said to have left everything and followed Jesus.

### Objectives

Learn about the call of the disciples.

Examine Judas' role in the betrayal of Jesus.

Begin to consider the disciples' role as leaders and role models for believers.

### Key terms

**Disciples**: a) followers of Jesus; b) the term is often used to refer to the first twelve followers of Jesus.

### Beliefs and teachings

An argument started among the disciples as to which of them would be the greatest. Jesus, knowing their thoughts, took a little child and had him stand beside him. Then he said to them, 'Whoever welcomes this little child in my name welcomes me; and whoever welcomes me welcomes the one who sent me. For he who is least among you all – he is the greatest.'

*Luke* 9:46–48

### AQA Examiner's tip

You will not be asked to list the names of the twelve.

If you read Luke 6:12–14 carefully, you will see that after a time of prayer Jesus was able to choose twelve disciples (he called them apostles) from among a larger group. These were: Peter, Andrew, James, John, Philip, Bartholomew, Matthew, Thomas, James the son of Alpheus, Simon the Zealot, Judas son of James and Judas Iscariot. All of them willingly followed Jesus.

The disciples sometimes quarrelled. In Luke 9:46–48 they were arguing about who was the greatest. Jesus told them to stop and to have more humility: 'For he who is least among you all – he is the greatest.'

A   *Fishermen of Galilee*

## Judas and the betrayal of Jesus

> *Now the Feast of Unleavened Bread, called the Passover, was approaching, and the chief priests and the teachers of the law were looking for some way to get rid of Jesus, for they were afraid of the people. Then Satan entered Judas, called Iscariot, one of the Twelve. And Judas went to the chief priests and the officers of the temple guard and discussed with them how he might betray Jesus. They were delighted and agreed to give him money. He consented, and watched for an opportunity to hand Jesus over to them when no crowd was present.*
>
> *Luke* 22:1–6

Judas took money from the chief priests for handing Jesus over to them. Luke mentions Satan as the cause of this.

Judas may have wanted Jesus to demonstrate that he was a political messiah. He did not show commitment to other disciples, or Jesus, in doing this.

## The disciples will be rewarded

> *You are those who have stood by me in my trials. And I confer on you a kingdom, just as my Father conferred one on me, so that you may eat and drink at my table in my kingdom and sit on thrones, judging the twelve tribes of Israel.*
>
> *Luke* 22:28–30

These statements of Jesus come after the disciples had been quarrelling about who was the greatest. Jesus knew that they were going to go through a difficult time and this was not the most important thing that they should be thinking about. They have stood by Jesus, and they all have authority as his disciples.

Jesus uses the idea of a banquet in heaven to emphasise that the disciples will be rewarded richly for their commitment. The disciples (including Judas at this stage) are promised that they will rule the kingdom. This of course is what the disciples were hoping for – a sense of authority – and is perhaps why they were arguing.

## ∞ links

Jesus was tempted by Satan in the desert (see pages 64–65).

### Activities

1. What do you think were the reasons why the disciples left everything to follow Jesus?
2. Why do you think Jesus chose disciples from groups that were unpopular, such as tax collectors and Zealots?
3. What does 'following Jesus' mean for Christians today?
4. Is it possible for modern believers to leave everything and follow Jesus?
5. Why do you think Judas handed over Jesus to the authorities?

### Summary

You will now know that Jesus called twelve disciples to follow him. This prompted an instant response and willingness to join the group, but Judas later betrayed him. Jesus taught that the disciples would have authority.

# 6.2    Peter (1)

## Peter in Luke's Gospel

Simon **Peter** was the first disciple called by Jesus. Peter was willing to lend to Jesus the boat that he was working in. The miraculous catch of fish convinced Peter that Jesus had power and he declared that Jesus should leave him alone because he was a sinner.

His original name was Simon, and Jesus named him Peter. This Greek name comes from 'petros', which means 'rock'. Jesus could see that Peter was like a rock and would be a very good leader for the church that would follow Jesus' work.

It is clear that Peter was impetuous and was often the first to do or say something – even if it was wrong.

Peter was present at all of the most important events in Luke's Gospel:

- When Jesus asked who had touched him in the healing of the woman with a haemorrhage, it was Peter who reminded Jesus that there was a crowd around him.
- Peter was also one of the three who entered Jairus' house. This gave him a very clear view of the powers that Jesus was demonstrating.
- Peter was the first to declare Jesus as 'The Christ'.
- A few days later Peter was a witness at the transfiguration, and it was he who wanted to build the booths.
- Peter was the one who pointed out to Jesus that the disciples had left everything to follow him.
- Peter was sent with John to prepare the Last Supper.
- After Jesus was arrested, Peter followed him, though at a distance, to the High Priest's house. There, he denied knowing Jesus.
- Peter was the first of the twelve disciples to go to the tomb after the women told what they had seen on the first Easter Sunday morning.

In Luke, Peter is the leading disciple – the one willing to take a risk and declare what he believed was true. He was able to experience moments of great spiritual insight. However, the account of Peter's denial of Jesus is preserved in all four gospels. It shows Peter as a frightened human being who could not, at this point, acknowledge that he was a follower of Jesus.

## Peter's promise

> 66 *Simon, Simon, Satan has asked to sift you as wheat. But I have prayed for you, Simon, that your faith may not fail. And when you have turned back, strengthen your brothers.' But he replied, 'Lord, I am ready to go with you to prison and to death.' Jesus answered, 'I tell you, Peter, before the rooster crows today, you will deny three times that you know me.* 99
>
> *Luke* 22:31–44

### Objectives

Learn about Jesus' warning to Peter that he would deny him.

Consider Peter as a role model for discipleship.

### Key terms

**Peter**: the leading apostle. Peter was the 'Rock' on which Jesus based the Church, and he was the first Pope.

### AQA    Examiner's tip

You will need to know this narrative and be able to retell it accurately. You may also be asked to come to a judgement on Peter's actions and give your reasons for thinking as you do.

### Beliefs and teachings

Jesus left the synagogue and went to the home of Simon. Now Simon's mother-in-law was suffering from a high fever, and they asked Jesus to help her. So he bent over her and rebuked the fever, and it left her. She got up at once and began to wait on them.

*Luke* 4:38–39

**A**   *St Peter Denying Jesus by Gustave Doré. Notice how sinister the crowd looks*

Jesus told Peter that he had prayed that Peter's faith would not fail him. Peter's task was to support his brother disciples and strengthen them. Typically it seems Peter said instantly that he was ready to go with Jesus.

Jesus knew that Peter's courage was going to fail him. He also knew that Peter would be very sorry for his actions and would go on to support the others.

The prediction from Jesus was very clear: 'before the rooster crows today you will deny three times that you know me'. Luke does not record a response from Peter.

## Satan

Having tempted Jesus in the desert, Satan disappeared until 'an opportune time' (Luke 4:13). Now Satan is mentioned again.

Luke has already stated that Judas was motivated by Satan to betray Jesus. Now Jesus himself tells Peter (called Simon in this passage) that Satan will test him.

# 6.3    Peter (2)

## ▌ 'I don't know him'

> Then seizing him, they led him away and took him into the house of the high priest. Peter followed at a distance. But when they had kindled a fire in the middle of the courtyard and had sat down together, Peter sat down with them. A servant girl saw him seated there in the firelight. She looked closely at him and said, 'This man was with him.' But he denied it. 'Woman, I don't know him,' he said.
>
> A little later someone else saw him and said, 'You also are one of them.' 'Man, I am not!' Peter replied.
>
> About an hour later another asserted, 'Certainly this fellow was with him, for he is a Galilean.' Peter replied, 'Man, I don't know what you're talking about!' Just as he was speaking, the rooster crowed. The Lord turned and looked straight at Peter. Then Peter remembered the word the Lord had spoken to him: 'Before the rooster crows today, you will disown me three times.' And he went outside and wept bitterly. "
>
> *Luke* 22:54–65

There is a parallel between Peter's denials and the temptation: there were three denials and three temptations. This account also emphasises how committed Jesus was and how weak Peter could be.

The fire would be lit in the courtyard because at that time of year it would be cold at night. By its light the servant girl and another two people were able to see Peter, and they also identified him by his **Galilean** accent. Peter didn't react very politely to the people who said they recognised him. He called the servant girl 'woman' and the other two people 'man'.

## ▌ Peter as a role model

Peter was a loyal and faithful disciple. He was with Jesus at all the key moments during Jesus' ministry and was one of his leading supporters. There is no doubt that Peter's faith in Jesus was well established – it was Peter who first recognised Jesus' real role, and he was willing to take the lead. So in these ways Peter is a good role model in Luke.

Later in his life, Peter took the lead in the Jerusalem Church, and when arrested he argued powerfully with the authorities that Jesus was the Messiah. There is evidence of healings done in his name. Eventually he persuaded the church to take its most radical step in allowing Gentiles to join.

### Objectives

Study the incident of Peter's denial.

Consider whether Peter was a good role model for Christians.

**A**   *Statue of St Peter in the Vatican*

Peter did make mistakes. This increases his relevance as a role model, because it shows that despite his importance he had human weaknesses. As far as we know, no other disciple was there when Peter denied knowing Jesus. He must have told that tale himself as part of his repentance.

Peter became the leader of the Church in Jerusalem after the Day of Pentecost and has been credited with writing the Letters of Peter in the New Testament. Tradition tells that he was eventually crucified in Rome. The Roman Catholic tradition regards him as the first Pope.

**B**  *Cross keys – the sign of St Peter*

## Peter's dream

In the Acts of the Apostles Peter had a dream in Joppa. In this dream he is told to kill and eat animals that would be considered unclean. God declares them clean, and Peter realises that Gentiles should be admitted to the church without first having to become Jewish believers and the men being circumcised (Acts 10:9–16).

**Activities**

1. Why do you think Peter followed Jesus to the High Priest's house?
2. What risk did he take?
3. How did the people recognise him?
4. In what ways might Christians today deny Jesus?

**Discussion activity**

If Christians were looking for a role model would they be wise to follow Peter's example?.

**Summary**

You will now know that Peter followed Jesus but denies three times that he knew him. Peter was a good role model for Christians in many ways.

# 6.4 Jesus' teaching about discipleship

## The call to be a disciple

When Jesus called the disciples he knew that it was not easy for them to follow him. He knew what was in store for him, and ultimately for the disciples if they kept faith. The early church faced real hardships of persecution.

### Would-be disciples

> ❝ As they were walking along the road, a man said to him, 'I will follow you wherever you go.' Jesus replied, 'Foxes have holes and birds of the air have nests, but the Son of Man has no place to lay his head.' He said to another man, 'Follow me.' But the man replied, 'Lord, first let me go and bury my father.' Jesus said to him, 'Let the dead bury their own dead, but you go and proclaim the kingdom of God.' Still another said, 'I will follow you, Lord; but first let me go back and say good-by to my family.' Jesus replied, 'No one who puts his hand to the plough and looks back is fit for service in the kingdom of God.' ❞
>
> *Luke* 9:57–62

### 'I will follow you wherever you go...'

Jesus' answer to this statement sounds almost like a proverb. Jesus accepted that most people, like animals, have homes to which they can return, but he knew that, for him, there was no home like that – there was no return. This would also be true for some of the disciples. The man said that he was ready to make a total commitment, but Luke does not tell us whether or not he followed Jesus.

### '...let me go and bury my father'

The second man hesitated. It seems harsh that Jesus would not give him time to do this, but for Jesus discipleship was all or nothing. In the Jewish religion, burying your parents was an important religious duty, and failure to do so was exceptionally disrespectful. Jesus would know that.

When Jesus said that the dead should bury their dead he was making the point that those who follow him are gaining new life. Those who do not follow are spiritually dead.

### '...first let me go back and say good-bye...'

In I Kings 19, Elisha asked Elijah if he could go back to kiss his mother and father before he followed him. Elijah agreed to this. For Jesus, however, there is no time for looking back.

## Christian discipleship

Disciples believe that God is with them and that the Holy Spirit will guide and protect them. They also adopt a pattern of living based on Jesus' teaching and the church's teaching.

### Objectives

Learn what Jesus said about discipleship.

Consider some examples of discipleship.

### Key terms

**Discipleship:** following Jesus during his lifetime. To be an active believer in Jesus.

**A** *Jesus said 'Take up your cross daily and follow me'*

### Extension activity

1. You could invite local Christians to school or college to explain what discipleship means to them.

## Paul the apostle

Saul had been at the stoning of Stephen and was going to Damascus to persecute Christians. On the way he saw a bright light, which blinded him, and heard the voice of Jesus (Acts 9:1–9). He became known as Paul and was a leader of the early church. Eventually he went to Rome with the Christian message, and to his certain death.

## William Booth

William Booth was the founder of the Salvation Army. He believed that the poor of Victorian Britain needed to become Christians and that something should be done about the social evils of their day. Despite being insulted and abused, the Salvation Army had a great effect on the lives of the poor. It is said that 55,000 people attended William Booth's funeral.

**B**   *Salvation Army at work*

> ### James Mawdsley
>
> *Case study*
>
> James Mawdsley was imprisoned in Burma during 1999 and 2000 for taking part in demonstrations in favour of democracy. While he was in prison he suffered abuse from the guards, although they claimed that he had injured himself. He was actually sentenced to seventeen years in prison but was released after the United Nations became involved. James Mawdsley's Christian beliefs meant that he felt he had to try to achieve justice for the Burmese people. As a committed Christian, he could not stand by and watch the government in Burma treat its people badly.
>
> A transcript of an interview with James by David Frost can be found at news.bbc.co.uk/1/hi/programmes/breakfast_with_frost/984646.stm .

## Nicky Cruz

Nicky Cruz was the leader of a notorious gang known as the Mau Maus in New York. He met a preacher, David Wilkerson. This preacher told Cruz that God loved him. Eventually Nicky became a Christian and began to preach the gospel around the world. His life story is told in the book *Run Baby Run*.

### Summary

You will now know Jesus' teaching on discipleship and what it would mean to be his follower. Many Christians have faced hardship in order to follow Jesus but like the early disciples, have found fulfilment in doing so.

### Activities

1. What does the strangers' willingness to follow Jesus show about Jesus' reputation?

2. Why do you think Jesus seemed to reject those who wanted to follow him?

3. Should people abandon their way of life to become disciples?

4. Is it right to encourage people to join a faith when it means them changing their life?

5. Why do Christians want to share their stories of conversion to the faith?

# 6.5 The Parable of the Rich Man and Lazarus

## The beggar at the gate

This parable is only in Luke's Gospel. It is an extremely powerful parable and has real meaning in the world today. If you visit some countries you will literally find at the gateway to hotels and rich mansions groups of people who have nothing and are perhaps homeless, with only makeshift tents to live in. The parable emphasises that following Jesus as a disciple does not just affect beliefs – there is a very practical aspect to it as well.

> ❝ There was a rich man who was dressed in purple and fine linen and lived in luxury every day. At his gate was laid a beggar named Lazarus, covered with sores and longing to eat what fell from the rich man's table. Even the dogs came and licked his sores. The time came when the beggar died and the angels carried him to Abraham's side. The rich man also died and was buried. In hell, where he was in torment, he looked up and saw Abraham far away, with Lazarus by his side. So he called to him, 'Father Abraham, have pity on me and send Lazarus to dip the tip of his finger in water and cool my tongue, because I am in agony in this fire.' But Abraham replied, 'Son, remember that in your lifetime you received your good things, while Lazarus received bad things, but now he is comforted here and you are in agony. And besides all this, between us and you a great chasm has been fixed, so that those who want to go from here to you cannot, nor can anyone cross over from there to us.' He answered, 'Then I beg you, father, send Lazarus to my father's house, for I have five brothers. Let him warn them, so that they will not also come to this place of torment.' Abraham replied, 'They have Moses and the Prophets; let them listen to them.' 'No, father Abraham,' he said, 'but if someone from the dead goes to them, they will repent.' He said to him, 'If they do not listen to Moses and the Prophets, they will not be convinced even if someone rises from the dead.' ❞
>
> *Luke* 16:19–31

### Objectives

Learn the Parable of the Rich Man and Lazarus.

Understand the interpretation of the parable.

Look at Christian responses to those in need around the world.

### Key terms

**Hell:** believed to be a place of unquenchable fire where sinners were sent for punishment after death.

### AQA Examiner's tip

You will need to be able to retell this parable accurately if you are asked.

**A** *Mumbai Shanty Town*

**B** *Mother Teresa of Calcutta*

## Interpreting the parable

The reversal of roles after death is a popular theme. This is a very Jewish version of it, with references to Abraham, Moses, **hell** and angels, for example. If people follow the teachings of Moses and the prophets, they will go to heaven – but the problem is, which teachings? Of the 613 rules in the Torah, which did Jesus mean? And which of the prophets? A likely explanation is that Jesus meant all the rules relating to how to treat those with nothing justly, and how to meet their needs.

The statement Jesus went on to make about people not listening even if someone rose from the dead is now seen as a clear reference to himself.

The importance of this parable lies in its obvious message: help those in need when you have the power or opportunity to do so, and do not be selfish with your possessions and money. It does not seem that being rich as such is condemned here.

There is also an indication in the parable of judgement and eternal rewards and punishment.

## Moses and the prophets

In the Old Testament there were strict rules about the way the poor, widows, orphans and strangers should be treated. Jews should look after the neediest, and foreigners were to be treated properly: the Jews had to remember that they were once foreigners.

Those with no means of producing food were to be given food from the tithes that were collected. During harvesting, if a sheaf was missed it had to be left for the orphans and widows to pick up. For the same reason olive trees were not to be beaten twice, or grapes picked twice.

Jesus' teaching stands in the tradition of the 8th century BCE prophets. Amos the prophet was actually a farmer who went to Bethel to tell the traders and religious leaders that they were to be condemned for their empty sacrifices and for cheating the poor. Jesus would have been well aware of this teaching.

## The Rich Man and Lazarus today

Today there are very rich nations and much poorer ones. This parable emphasises the obligation that Christians feel to less economically developed countries and their needs. Christians do not want the poor to be invisible and ignored.

The motivation for many organisations and individuals today is to meet the needs of the poorest people. This is the response that the Rich Man should have made, but did not.

### Summary

You will now know the parable of the Rich Man and Lazarus, which teaches the importance of caring for the poor. Christians today are challenged to address the problem of poverty in many countries across the world.

### Mother Teresa

Mother Teresa of Calcutta is one of the most famous workers for those in need that the world has ever known. She was Albanian by birth and founded a religious order, the Missionaries of Charity, in 1950. Until her death in 2005, Mother Teresa worked with the poorest children in Calcutta, feeding them and ensuring that they had medical care and food. Mother Teresa's commitment as a Christian disciple has led the Roman Catholic Church to begin the process of making her a saint.

'In the example of Blessed Teresa of Calcutta we have a clear illustration of the fact that time devoted to God in prayer not only does not detract from effective and loving service to our neighbour but is in fact the inexhaustible source of that service.' (Pope Benedict VI)

*www.motherteresa.org*

### Research activity

Do a web search on the work of Sister Emmanuel of Cairo who worked with the children on the rubbish dumps.

www.martinfrost.ws/htmlfiles/oct2008/sister-emmanuelle.html

### Activities

1. How do you know that the rich man was very rich?
2. What could the poor man have done to help himself?
3. Why did Abraham refuse the requests of the Rich Man?
4. What does this parable teach about discipleship?
5. 'Charity begins at home.' Do you agree? Give reasons for your answer.

### Eternal life

> A certain ruler asked him, 'Good teacher, what must I do to inherit eternal life?' 'Why do you call me good?' Jesus answered. 'No one is good – except God alone. You know the commandments: "Do not commit adultery, do not murder, do not steal, do not give false testimony, honour your father and mother."'
>
> 'All these I have kept since I was a boy,' he said. When Jesus heard this, he said to him, 'You still lack one thing. Sell everything you have and give to the poor, and you will have treasure in heaven. Then come, follow me.' When he heard this, he became very sad, because he was a man of great wealth. Jesus looked at him and said, 'How hard it is for the rich to enter the kingdom of God! Indeed, it is easier for a camel to go through the eye of a needle than for a rich man to enter the kingdom of God.' Those who heard this asked, 'Who then can be saved?' Jesus replied, 'What is impossible with men is possible with God.' Peter said to him, 'We have left all we had to follow you!' 'I tell you the truth,' Jesus said to them, 'no one who has left home or wife or brothers or parents or children for the sake of the kingdom of God will fail to receive many times as much in this age and, in the age to come, eternal life.'
>
> *Luke* 18:18–30

### Objectives

Learn the story of the rich ruler.

Identify how Jesus uses the incident to teach about riches.

### AQA Examiner's tip

You need to be able to retell this incident accurately. You also need to be able to use the teaching of Jesus and the conversation with the disciples to illustrate answers on riches and discipleship.

### 'What must I do to inherit eternal life?'

This was a question that could have been addressed to any teacher at the time. Jesus asked why the man called him 'good', when only God is good.

As a 'son of the Covenant' the rich man would have gone though his bar mitzvah at about the age of thirteen. At that point he would have been responsible for keeping the law. Jesus stressed that the way to eternal life and heaven is to keep the commandments.

Jesus was concerned for the needs of those less well off than the rich man. The man could not make the commitment needed to follow Jesus.

### Riches and the Kingdom

Some interpreters have suggested that when Jesus referred to a camel going through the eye of a needle he was referring to the small pedestrian-only gate in the city wall. A camel would have difficulty going though this small gate. Others have said that this statement should be taken more literally. Jesus was making the point that it was very hard for those with riches to get close to God – so hard, that to make the point he used the absurd idea of a camel going through the eye of a needle.

### links

See page 31 to remind yourself of the way Sylvia Wright understood this parable to relate to her.

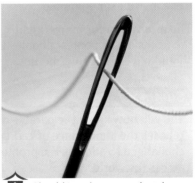

**A** *Should Jesus' comment be taken literally?*

**B**   *A loaded camel would have had to be unpacked to get through the city gate*

There is no doubt that the rich young ruler would have been greatly disappointed by Jesus' words. It may even be that he was shocked because he believed he had done the right things all his life. Jesus knew that faith is crucial, and being obsessed by possessions can get in the way of faith.

## Peter's response

Peter reminded Jesus that the disciples had left everything to follow him. Jesus told them again that their commitment would be rewarded many times over, and that they would receive eternal life. Whether Christian disciples are motivated by this promise is doubtful. Discipleship is about commitment and service – there is rarely a reward. Christian disciples are motivated by their desire to love others and serve them.

**C**   *For some people money is everything*

### Activities

1   What answer do you think the rich young ruler expected Jesus to give when he said he had kept the commandments?

2   Why would he have been shocked by the answer he received?

3   What do you think the phrase about the camel not going through the eye of a needle means?

4   Why did Peter ask about giving everything up to follow Jesus?

5   'It is hard to pray when your fridge is full.' Do you agree? Give reasons for your answer.

### Discussion activity

How easy is it for Christians to teach people in the world today that there is a heaven?

### Summary

You will now know the rich young ruler had kept all the commandments, but his riches stood in the way of faith. Here Jesus suggests that possessions can be a barrier to discipleship.

## 6.7 Prayer

### ■ The Parable of the Persistent Neighbour

> Then he said to them, 'Suppose one of you has a friend, and he goes to him at midnight and says, "Friend, lend me three loaves of bread, because a friend of mine on a journey has come to me, and I have nothing to set before him."
>
> 'Then the one inside answers, "Don't bother me. The door is already locked, and my children are with me in bed. I can't get up and give you anything." I tell you, though he will not get up and give him the bread because he is his friend, yet because of the man's boldness he will get up and give him as much as he needs.'
>
> *Luke* 11:5–8

### Objectives

Study the Parable of the Persistent Neighbour.

Examine the teaching in Luke about prayer.

Understand what prayer means for Christian discipleship.

### Key terms

**Prayer:** communication with God through words of praise, thanks or sorrow, or requests for his help or guidance. Luke's Gospel refers to Jesus praying on a number of occasions.

In this parable Jesus illustrates very clearly what **prayer** means. Security was important in those days and once someone had closed up their house for the night, they were very reluctant to open it again. Yet the neighbour came and asked for bread because a visitor had arrived and he had a duty to feed him. He was persistent, and eventually he got the bread he wanted.

In this short parable Jesus is saying that people must be persistent in prayer, and that God will answer prayer just as the friend answered his neighbour.

### ■ What is prayer?

Following this parable, Jesus gives two more examples of what prayer is like:

- If they knock, the door will be opened; if they search, they will find (Luke 11:9–10). People should have faith that whatever they ask for they will receive.
- People would not give a child a snake if he asked for a fish, or a scorpion if he asked for an egg (Luke 11:11–13). God is seen by believers to give people what they need.

William Temple, a former Archbishop of Canterbury, on being told that answered prayer was a coincidence, replied, 'That may be true, but I've noticed that when I pray coincidences happen and when I don't, they don't.'

Prayer is the way in which humans feel that they are communicating with God and is part of almost every religion. It is an important theme in Luke's Gospel.

Jesus is recorded many times praying himself and encouraging others to pray. The word occurs in one form or another some 22 times in Luke. At least seven of these references are found only in Luke.

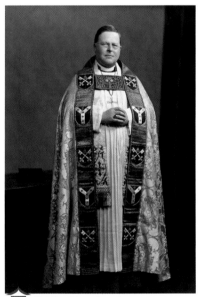

**A** *William Temple, a former Archbishop of Canterbury*

### ∞ links

There is further teaching on prayer and discipleship in the Parable of the Pharisee and the Tax Collector (see pages 134–135).

**B**   *People at prayer*

## Jesus at prayer

Jesus is described as praying at crucial times in his life.

- He is shown to pray alone on the mountain.
- On one occasion we are told that he had prayed all night.
- On the Mount of Olives he prayed that he would not have to face the coming events.
- In his teaching on prayer, Jesus told the disciples to pray for strength from God and taught them how to pray using what has become known as the Lord's Prayer.

## Prayer in the time of Jesus

There was a strong tradition in Judaism that God would answer prayer. God was seen as one who answered the prayers of the faithful. In the Jewish mind prayer was linked to sacrifice.

Jewish prayers had a pattern, usually beginning with a phrase of praise to God and ending with a blessing. The Hebrew word 'amen', which appears at the end of prayers, means 'we say this together faithfully'.

From the 1st century BCE there are prayers preserved in the Dead Sea Scrolls. There are some 90 prayers in the Bible and they range from individual requests to formal prayers on behalf of the whole nation.

It is against this background that Jesus taught and set an example of prayer as a major part of life.

**⚭ links**

You can read about the Lord's Prayer on pages 132–133.

**Activities**

1. What is prayer?
2. How did Jesus set an example for prayer?
3. Do people only pray when they have no other options left?
4. If prayer is not answered, does this mean that God does not exist?
5. What can Christians learn about prayer and discipleship from the Parable of the Persistent Neighbour?

## The Lord's Prayer

### Beliefs and teachings

One day Jesus was praying in a certain place. When he finished, one of his disciples said to him, 'Lord, teach us to pray, just as John taught his disciples.' He said to them, 'When you pray, say:

"Father,
  hallowed be your name,
  your kingdom come.
  Give us each day our daily bread.
  Forgive us our sins,
  for we also forgive everyone who sins against us.
  And lead us not into temptation."

*Luke* 11:1–8

The Lord's Prayer is shorter in Luke than in Matthew. It is quite likely that Jesus taught it on more than one occasion. Many of the phrases used in this prayer are found in other Jewish prayers. The Lord's Prayer has become one of the central prayers of Christian worship throughout the world. It is used in many different Christian services.

The prayer may not have been taught to be memorised and used over and over again as it is now. It may have been a model that Jesus gave to the disciples to help them shape their own prayers. He may have said, 'This is the sort of thing you should pray…'

### 'Father'

The Greek (and Latin) for Father is 'pater', which can translate to the Aramaic word 'abba'. Jesus would have spoken Aramaic. God is described as a father figure, and in this version of the prayer it is the term that a child would use – almost like 'daddy'. Jesus was so close to God that he could call him by that name. God is not a distant judge and rule-setter, and Jesus, as the Son of God, can address God very personally.

### 'Hallowed be your name'

It was quite wrong of any Jew to pronounce the name of God. 'Hallowed' means holy. For a Jew, something holy was set aside and dedicated to God. So God's name was sacred.

### 'Your kingdom come'

This could refer to the idea of heaven at the end of time. It could also be a request for the Kingdom of God to exist on earth in the way people act in this world.

### 'Give us each day our daily bread'

Up to now the person praying has been addressing God and praying that God's power will be at work in the world. Now there is a

### Objectives

Study some of Jesus' teaching on prayer.

Know and understand the Lord's Prayer.

Think about the use of the Lord's Prayer in public and private worship.

### Discussion activity

Discuss what your own views on prayer are with others in your group. Why do you think some prayers seem to be answered and others not?

straightforward request for food. This could be a request for actual food itself, or 'daily bread' could more generally mean all that is needed for us to live from day to day.

### 'Forgive us our sins'

This is an important part of Jesus' teaching in Luke, and it is at the heart of the prayer. Christians are also expected to be forgiving people.

### 'Lead us not into temptation'

This is the only request that has a negative in it. It can also be translated as 'do not bring us to the test'. For the early Christians this would bring hope that God might somehow spare them from the trials and tribulations of the persecutions that they faced. It also could mean that they did not want to be tempted as Jesus was. They would certainly pray that they might not be tempted more than they could bear.

### ◼ The Lord's Prayer in worship

The Lord's Prayer is used in public worship. It is seen as a prayer that unites all Christians from every denomination. It can be said by a group of worshippers in a church, or an individual can use the Lord's Prayer in private worship. In some versions of the Rosary, Roman Catholic worshippers say the Lord's Prayer as part of their own prayers.

Christian disciples use the prayer to remind them of their commitment to God. They are expressing their adoration for God and the confidence that they have in his work in the world. They are also asking God for the things they need. As disciples they are acknowledging God's presence with them, particularly if they face trouble.

**A** *Jewish prayer at the Western Wall in Jersualem where Jews have prayed since the time of Jesus*

**AQA** *Examiner's tip*

Learn Luke's version of the Lord's Prayer for the examination.

**Research activity** ⭕⬎

Find some muscial versions of the Lord's Prayer and listen to them.

Do they make it easier to understand?

**Activities**

1. Is it right for people to pray for their earthly needs?

2. Who gains most from forgiveness, the forgiver or the forgiven?

3. 'Prayer is a mark of discipleship.' Do you agree? Give reasons for your answer.

### Summary

You will now know that Jesus taught his disciples the Lord's Prayer, perhaps as a model on which they could base other prayers. Today most Christians use this prayer both publicly and privately.

### The Pharisee's prayer

> 66 *To some who were confident of their own righteousness and looked down on everybody else, Jesus told this parable: 'Two men went up to the temple to pray, one a Pharisee and the other a tax collector. The Pharisee stood up and prayed about himself: "God, I thank you that I am not like other men – robbers, evildoers, adulterers – or even like this tax collector. I fast twice a week and give a tenth of all I get."*
>
> *'But the tax collector stood at a distance. He would not even look up to heaven, but beat his breast and said "God, have mercy on me, a sinner."*
>
> *'I tell you that this man, rather than the other, went home justified before God. For everyone who exalts himself will be humbled, and he who humbles himself will be exalted.'* 99
>
> *Luke* 18:9–14

**Objectives**

Study the Parable of the Pharisee and the Tax Collector.

Understand what it teaches about repentance and forgiveness.

**Key terms**

**Pharisees**: devout Jewish religious leaders whose lives centred around the keeping of the Jewish Law. They came into conflict with Jesus many times on matters relating to the law.

**AQA** *Examiner's tip*

You will need to know this parable and what it teaches about the importance of prayer for Christian discipleship.

Jesus could be accused of stereotyping in this parable. He was using the **Pharisee** as an example of a self-righteous man of God looking down on a tax collector. This interpretation misses the main teaching in the parable, which is about repentance and sincerity in prayer. God will forgive those who repent.

The parable is set in the Temple, the most holy place for the Jewish people. Many believed that God was at home there. This setting makes the parable seem more important.

### The Pharisee

The Pharisee is shown as claiming to be worthy of worshipping God and to be much better than the tax collector. He referred to the laws that he kept by fasting twice a week and paying tithes on all he received. He listed the things that he was not: a robber, an evildoer, an adulterer. He was certain that he was not like the tax collector.

### The tax collector

In contrast, the tax collector stayed back. He did not dare to look up to heaven and he beat his breast. This is a rare reference in Jewish and early Christian writings to a symbolic action that was used to show sorrow. He recognises that he is a sinner.

### Jesus' message

Yet Jesus again challenged his hearers by saying that it was the tax collector who went home justified and forgiven. Humility is what counted, and he had demonstrated that he was aware of his wrong-doing.

There is wit and challenge in this story. It can be said that both men were religious. They were both ready to approach God in prayer.

**Beliefs and teachings**

Then Jesus told his disciples a parable to show them that they should always pray and not give up. [2]He said: 'In a certain town there was a judge who neither feared God nor cared about men. [3]And there was a widow in that town who kept coming to him with the plea, "Grant me justice against my adversary."

[4]'For some time he refused. But finally he said to himself, "Even though I don't fear God or care about men, [5]yet because this widow keeps bothering me, I will see that she gets justice, so that she won't eventually wear me out with her coming!"'

*Luke* 18:1–5

**A** *A picture of the Pharisee and the Tax Collector*

The Pharisee, though, was more interested in himself than in God. Jesus' hearers would have been disappointed by the Pharisee and surprised at the tax collector.

### Other teachings of Jesus on Prayer

- In the Parable of The Widow and the Unjust Judge (Luke 18:1–5), the woman is so persistent that the judge gives in to her demands. In all the parables he told on prayer – The Pharisee and the Tax Collector, the Persistent Neighbour and the Widow and the Unjust Judge – Jesus is putting over three main points:

- God can be approached at any time.

- God will respond to those who pray – but not necessarily immediately.

- God accepts the prayers of those who are repentant and confess their sins.

**AQA   *Examiner's tip***

You will not be asked to recall the Parable of the Widow and the Unjust Judge.

**⚭ links**

You can read the Parable of the Persistent Neighbour on pages 130–131.

**Extension activity**

Read the Parable of the Widow and the Unjust Judge (Luke 18:1–5). How does this parable fit Jesus' general teaching about prayer?

**Activities**

1. How did the Pharisee indicate that he was superior to others?
2. Why did the Tax Collector stand back?
3. What did Jesus want his hearers to understand about prayer in this parable?
4. This parable is like the parable of the Good Samaritan in some ways. Try to identify the ways in which the parables are similar.
5. What can Christians learn from Jesus' parables about prayer?

**Summary**

You will now know that Jesus taught the Parable of the Pharisee and the Tax Collector in order to teach his disciples about the importance of repentance and humility in prayer.

## Becoming a disciple

> 66 *Jesus promised His disciples three things: that they would be entirely fearless, absurdly happy, and that they would get into trouble.* 99
>
> W. Russell Maltby

The word 'disciple' means a 'learner' or a 'pupil'. We use it to mean 'follower' as well. **The twelve** were not the only disciples that Jesus had. Luke refers to 72 disciples being sent by Jesus to preach, teach and heal (Luke 10:1–16). There were also women followers.

### A way of life

Discipleship is a way of life. When Jesus asked the twelve to follow him, he changed their lives forever. They continued to do ordinary things. They went back to fishing from time to time. But they changed their priorities, and spent time travelling and listening to Jesus.

They found themselves in difficult situations, and later, after Jesus had died and the Resurrection had taken place, they were told by Jesus what was expected of them: they should follow Jesus, preach the gospel and be prepared to suffer for it.

Jesus never pretended that they had made an easy choice. The life of discipleship brought great rewards, but also brought problems.

### What to expect

Luke says that the disciples were expected to:

- give up everything, and rely on faith to survive
- share the message of God and call for people to repent of their sins
- be prepared to not always be welcomed by people
- heal the sick, drive out evil spirits
- become leaders of the community of those who followed Jesus
- set an example to others of following the message of the Kingdom of God
- suffer for their faith – there is an element of sacrifice in discipleship
- demonstrate humility and be above petty human squabbles about position
- pray for strength to fulfil their calling.

## What happened to the disciples?

Many of the disciples went out to preach the gospel. Luke tells that on the Day of Pentecost there was a sound of wind and it appeared that tongues of fire were touching the disciples' heads (Acts 2). They then came out onto the streets of Jerusalem, preaching Jesus the Messiah – risen from the dead. This led them into conflict with the Jews and eventually also with the Romans.

A Discipleship is a way of life

**B**  *Death of St Andrew*

## Legends and traditions

What happened to the twelve is preserved in the legends which were passed around the early church and written up.

- Peter is said to have been crucified upside down in Rome, in about 64 CE.
- Thomas went to India. He was arrested for preaching Christianity and converting people, and a soldier killed him with a spear.
- Andrew is thought to have been crucified (a very late tradition says it was on a saltire cross, shaped like an 'X').
- Bartholomew is said to have been skinned alive with the sort of flaying knife used by tanners to prepare leather.

## ■ A legacy

Whatever happened to them, they left a legacy that was to be world-changing. They were the only ones who could continue Jesus' work.

Christian followers today feel that their calling is just the same as that of the first disciples – to preach the gospel and share it with others. They have a strong sense of their responsibility to live out the life of discipleship and to share the gospel in their own community. For some this includes suffering.

**Activities**

1  What does the word 'disciple' mean?

2  What did Jesus expect of his disciples?

3  What do you think motivated the disciples to follow Jesus?

4  Do you think that discipleship was easier at the time of Jesus?

5  'Christian discipleship has no value today.' Do you agree? Give reasons for your answer.

**Summary**

You will now understand that Christian discipleships – following the example of the twelve disciples – is a way of life. Luke gives many examples of what this way of life might involve.

6

## Discipleship – summary

For the examination you should now be able to:

✓ explain the key elements of Christian discipleship

✓ recount the call of the first disciples and understand how the twelve are seen as role models by Christians today

✓ understand the influence and function of modern leaders and celebrities as role models for Christians

✓ recognise the costs and demands of discipleship

✓ know about Jesus' teaching on wealth and possessions and the importance of that message for society today

✓ describe and explain the Parable of the Rich Man and Lazarus and the incident involving the rich young ruler

✓ be able to retell two parables about prayer

✓ understand the Lord's Prayer, the centrality of prayer in the life and teaching of Jesus and its importance for Christian discipleship.

### Sample answer

1. Read the following examination question:

'The demands that Jesus made on his disciples were unfair.' Do you agree? Give reasons for your answer, showing that you have thought about it from more than one point of view? *(6 marks)*

2. Read the sample answer below.

'Jesus called twelve men to be his disciples. There were others and at one point there is a reference to seventy-two disciples. Jesus expected his disciples to give up everything. This might have been seen as fair for some disciples but others did not think this. In the incident of the rich young ruler Jesus told him to sell everything that he had and to follow him. The rich young ruler could not do this and so did not follow Jesus. He clearly thought that Jesus' demands were unfair.

Jesus though promised his disciples a reward. He said that they would be in heaven and act as judges and share in a banquet. The disciples would have seen this as a reward for their commitment to following Jesus. This would have been seen as a very fair balance for them. However it is clear that the disciples were expected to give up their lifestyles and leave their families. I think this is unfair because it is possible to be a disciple today and stay with your family.'

3. With a partner, discuss the sample answer. Do you think there are things that could be added or taken out?

4. How many marks would you give this out of 6? Look at the mark scheme in the Introduction on page 7 (AO2).What are the reasons for the mark you have given?

# AQA Examination-style questions

Look at this picture and answer the following questions.

 **Examiner's tip**  In this first group of questions you need to know the text of Luke well.

1    What did Jesus usually say when he called the first disciples?    *(2 marks)*

2    How did Jesus first demonstrate his power to Peter?    *(2 marks)*

3    Why did Judas hand Jesus over to the authorities?    *(3 marks)*

4    Describe the Parable of the Pharisee and the Tax Collector.    *(4 marks)*

5    What can Christians learn from Parable of the Rich Man and Lazarus?    *(4 marks)*

**AQA Examiner's tip**  These questions require you to show that you know Luke's Gospel and show that you understand some of the meanings.

6    Explain why the rich young ruler was not able to follow Jesus.    *(4 marks)*

7    What did Jesus teach about persistence in prayer?    *(5 marks)*

**AQA Examiner's tip**  Do not just retell a parable in this answer. Refer to more than one.

8    'Christian discipleship is just too difficult today – it was much easier for the first disciples.' Do you agree? Give reasons for your answer, showing that you have thought about more than one point of view.    *(6 marks)*

9    What can Christians learn from Peter's denial of Jesus?    *(6 marks)*

**AQA Examiner's tip**  Notice that the question asks 'What can Christians learn from...' Do not just tell the story.

10    'Without prayer no one can be a Christian.' Do you agree? Give reasons for your answer, showing that you have thought about more than one point of view.    *(6 marks)*

# Glossary

## A

**Angel:** a messenger from God.

**Annunciation:** the name given to the occasion when the angel Gabriel appeared in a vision to Mary, telling her that she was to conceive and give birth to the Son of God.

**Anointing:** oil was poured on the head of Israelite kings at their coronation as a sign that they were chosen by God, and it came to have Messianic significance. The Hebrew term Messiah means 'anointed one'.

**Apostles:** the first 12 disciples of Jesus who became the leaders of the early church. The word means 'sent out'.

**Aramaic:** the language spoken by Jesus.

**Authority:** power to give orders to others and expect obedience.

## B

**Baptism:** a) the sacrament through which people become members of the church; b) in Luke's Gospel, John the Baptist used baptism as a way of washing away sins in readiness for the coming of the Messiah. He also baptised Jesus, though this was not connected with the washing away of sin.

**Bethlehem:** also known as the City of David. The birthplace of King David and the predicted birth place of the Messiah in the Old Testament.

**Bible:** sacred book for Christians containing both the Old and New Testaments.

**Blasphemy:** a) claiming to be God or equal with God; b) using God's name in a disrespectful way.

## C

**Centurion:** an important officer in the Roman Army. A centurion was present at Jesus' crucifixion.

**Christ:** the leader promised by God to the Jews. The word literally means 'Anointed One' in Greek; the Hebrew equivalent is Messiah. Christians believe Jesus to be the Christ.

**Christian:** someone who believes in Jesus Christ and follows the religion based on his teaching.

**Commandment:** a) a rule for living, given by God; b) one of the Ten Commandments; c) Jesus said that the greatest Commandments were love of God and of neighbour.

**Crucifixion:** Roman method of execution by which criminals were fixed to a cross. The execution and death of Jesus on Good Friday.

## D

**Debtor:** one who owes money to another.

**Disciples:** a) followers of Jesus; b) the term is often used to refer to the first twelve followers of Jesus.

**Discipleship:** following Jesus during his lifetime. To be an active believer in Jesus.

**Discrimination:** to treat someone or something differently either favouring or denying something, e.g. not allowing lepers to be part of the community.

## E

**Elijah:** an Old Testament prophet. It was believed that he would come to help the good people in trouble and return to prepare the way for the Messiah.

**Equality:** treating every person in a way that ensures justice and fairness.

**Eyewitness:** one who was alive and witnessed for themselves some of the events in Jesus' life.

## F

**Faith:** belief and trust in someone, for example, Jesus.

**Forgiveness:** to pardon a person for something that they have done wrong. In Biblical times, it was believed that only God could forgive sins.

## G

**Galilean:** one from Galilee where Jesus was brought up and recognised by a distinctive accent.

**Gentile:** a non-Jewish person.

**Gospel:** literally 'Good News'; there are four gospels telling of the life and work of Jesus.

## H

**Haemorrhage:** severe loss of blood.

**Hebrew:** the language in which most of the Jewish scriptures were written.

**Hell:** believed to be a place of unquenchable fire where sinners were sent for punishment after death.

**Herod Antipas:** the ruler of Galilee and Peraea at the time of Jesus' ministry. Pilate sent Jesus to Herod for trial.

**High Priest:** the High Priest was a special figure in the Jerusalem Temple. He often was also the leader of the Sanhedrin, the supreme council of the Jews. The High Priest who condemned Jesus to death was called Caiaphas.

**Holy Spirit:** the third person of the Holy Trinity who descended like a dove on Jesus at his baptism. Chistians believe that the Holy Spirit is present and inspires them.

## J

**Jesus:** 1st-century Jewish teacher and holy man, believed by Christians to be the Son of God.

**Jewish council (Sanhedrin):** the Supreme Council of the Jews consisted of 71 members, usually led by the High Priest, and who met in Jerusalem.

**Justice:** the bringing about of what is right, fair, according to the law, or making up for what has been done wrong.

## K

**Kingdom of God:** wherever God is honoured as king and his authority accepted. Jesus taught about the Kingdom of God both on earth and in heaven. The rule of God.

## L

**L:** refers to the material that is unique to Luke's Gospel. This material probably came from a variety of sources, oral and written.

**Last Supper:** the final meal that Jesus ate with his disciples, on the evening before his execution. It was based on the Jewish Passover and is the basis of Holy Communion today.

**Lord:** this was the messianic title given to Jesus by the early Church after his resurrection. By the time Luke wrote his Gospel, the title was in common use, so Luke uses it.

**Luke:** the Gospel is anonymous, but there are several things that support the early Christian tradition that the author was the physician, Luke, who was a Gentile convert (see 'Gentiles') and friend of Paul (Colossians 4:14; 2 Timothy 4:11; Philemon 24). The Gospel seems to have been written during the last third of the 1st century CE.

## M

**Mark's Gospel:** believed to be one of the sources used by Luke when writing his gospel.

**Materialist:** used to describe someone who has a great interest in possessions, money and wealth.

**Messiah:** the person whom God will send to save humanity, believed by Christians to be Jesus (the Anointed One). Hebrew form of the word Christ.

**Miracle:** an event that lies beyond normal human knowledge and understanding. It is an unexpected event with religious significance.

**Moses:** the man who rescued the Jews from Egypt and received the Ten Commandments from God.

**Mount of Olives:** the hilly area outside Jerusalem that consisted of olive orchards. This was where Jesus spent time in prayer after the last supper and where he was arrested.

## N

**Nazareth:** the town in Galilee in which Jesus was brought up.

## P

**Parables:** stories told by Jesus that have spiritual meanings.

**The Passion:** the term used to describe Jesus' suffering prior to his death.

**Paul:** Paul travelled through Asia Minor, Cyprus and Greece, preaching the gospel. Luke is thought to have accompanied Paul on some of his missionary journeys.

**Pharisees:** devout Jewish religious leaders whose lives centred around the keeping of the Jewish Law. They came into conflict with Jesus many times on matters relating to the law.

**Pilate:** the Roman governor of Judaea at the time of Jesus' ministry. Only he could give the death penalty, and so the Jewish council took Jesus to Pilate for trial.

**Prayer:** communication with God through words of praise, thanks or sorrow, or requests for his help or guidance. Luke's Gospel refers to Jesus praying on a number of occasions.

**Peter:** the leading apostle. Peter was the 'Rock' on which Jesus based the Church, and he was the first Pope.

**Pontius Pilate:** the Roman Governor of Palestine and the Emperor's representative.

**Prejudice:** to be in favour of, or to be against, someone or something without evidence. To pre-judge.

## Q

**Q:** a symbol standing for the German word 'Quelle' ('source'). It refers to the material, largely teaching, that many scholars think both Matthew and Luke used for their gospels.

## R

**Religious experience:** the belief that you have been directly contacted or spoken to by God/Jesus.

**Repentance:** saying sorry and acknowledging to God that a believer has done wrong.

**The Resurrection:** when Jesus rose from the dead after dying on the Cross. One of the key beliefs of Christianity.

**Revelation:** an experience or gift of enlightenment, specifically from God. The old priest Simeon spoke of Jesus as a light bringing revelation to the Gentiles.

**role models:** people who others follow and try to copy in their actions or beliefs.

## S

**Sabbath:** the Jewish day of rest, from sunset on Friday to sunset on Saturday.

**Salvation:** saving the soul, deliverance from sin and admission to heaven brought about by Jesus.

**Salvation history:** the story of Jesus is presented from the perspective of faith in him as sent by God to save humanity.

**Samaritans:** the Samaritans were mixed-race Jews. They regarded each other as enemies, so in Luke's Parable of the Good Samaritan, the Samaritan had no obligation to help the injured Jew.

**Satan:** the evil force that tempts people, also known as the devil.

**Saviour:** Christians believe that in his life and death, Jesus set people free from the power of evil and sin.

**Scribes:** known as 'doctors of the Law', they were the experts in the Jewish Law at the time of Jesus.

**Secular:** a set of beliefs which does not need to have God or religion in them.

**Son of David:** a title used for Jesus. Christians believe that Jesus fulfilled the Old Testament prophecy that the Messiah would be a descendant of King David.

**Son of God:** a title used for Jesus. The second person of the Trinity; denotes the special relationship between Jesus and God. Christians believe that before his birth as a human being, Jesus always existed as God the Son. Also means a righteous man.

**Son of Man:** a title used by Jesus of himself. In the Old Testament, the title was used of a heavenly being from God. Jesus used the title to stress that he was more than simply a human being and that he came with authority from God. Jesus also linked the title with suffering and service.

**Source:** a text, statement, or person that supplies information.

**Sunday:** the first day of the week in the Jewish religion. The day that Christians keep as holy to remember the Resurrection of Jesus.

**Synagogue:** where Jews meet for worship on the Sabbath. Jews regularly attended the synagogue.

**Synoptic:** literally, 'with one eye', this refers to the Gospels of Matthew, Mark and Luke, because of the similarities between them.

### T

**Tax collector:** these were despised because they were dishonest, did not keep ritual laws and worked for the Romans.

**Temptation:** a test of faith; being attracted to act in a wrong way, or being tested through suffering.

**The devil:** the evil force that tempts people, also known as Satan.

**Theophilus:** the gospel is addressed (Luke 1:3) to Theophilus, an unknown Christian, and perhaps socially prominent (hence the title, 'most excellent', which Luke uses of another high-ranking person in Acts 23 26).

**The Temple:** the most holy place of the Jews, built in Jerusalem and the centre of their worship. It was destroyed by the Romans in 70 CE.

**The temptations:** Jesus, while free from sin, was still subject to every form of temptation that humans face, including fear, doubt, depression, reluctance and lust.

**The twelve:** the twelve men chosen by Jesus to help with his ministry.

**Transfiguration:** an incident in the New Testament when Jesus was lit up by divine light, through which the divinity of Jesus was revealed.

### U

**Universalism:** a central theme in Luke's Gospel. It refers to Jesus' acceptance of everyone, including those depised and look down on by most people.

### V

**Vocation:** feeling called by God to take a particular course of action.

### W

**Widow:** a woman whose husband had died. In Jesus' time they had little support apart from their family.

### Z

**Zealots:** Jewish revolutionaries who plotted violent rebellion against the Romans. One of the twelve was Simon the Zealot and others may have been Zealots, but Jesus' teaching rejected their ideas on violence.